Praise for *Reignite Your Power*

"A must-read compassionate and empowering guide to healing trauma."
—Peter A Levine, PhD, developer of Somatic Experiencing® and an international best-selling author of *Waking the Tiger, Healing Trauma*

"This is a user-friendly book, straightforward, simple and helpful. It shows us how to understand our difficulties and teaches us how to move from trauma to love."
—Jack Kornfield, PhD, author of *A Path with Heart: A Guide Through the Perils and Promises of Spiritual Life*

"This extremely helpful book gives you a deep understanding of stress and trauma, many practical tools, deep contemplative insights, and the warm and supportive guidance of its author. This is a rare combination—and a gem of a book."
—Rick Hanson, PhD, author of *Buddha's Brain, Hardwiring Happiness, Resilient* and *Neurodharma*.

"Carefully crafted to gently guide readers in their learning and deepening of mindfulness practices, *Reignite Your Power* is a blend of ancient wisdom, Western science, and simple—yet powerful—mindfulness practices. It is that rare book which manages to be equally informative for a range of readers: the novice who has no previous experience with mindfulness or trauma recovery practices; those well along in their healing journey; and the seasoned practitioner.
Bareja weaves threads drawn from different knowledge traditions into a cohesive whole, and then distills that information into simple, effective, and well-considered practices for the reader to use in daily life. Stories drawn from Bareja's teaching and practice bring further clarity to the practical application of the tools presented in each chapter."

—Kathy L. Kain, PhD, co-author of *Nurturing Resilience: Helping Clients Move Forward from Developmental Trauma* and *The Tao of Trauma: A Practitioner's Guide for Integrating Five Element Theory and Trauma Treatment*

"*Reignite Your Power* is a deeply compassionate guide for anyone ready to face the impact of trauma and step into lasting resilience. Drawing from a rich lineage of spiritual practice, embodied mindfulness, and decades of trauma-informed teaching, Pawan Bareja offers readers powerful tools for transformation. Using stories from clients and her own journey, Dr. Bareja invites us to meet trauma not as an enemy but as a teacher, showing how even our most painful experiences can become portals to aliveness, love, and belonging."
—David Treleaven, PhD, author of *Trauma-Sensitive Mindfulness: Practices for Safe and Transformative Healing*

"A good balance of spirituality and practical application, this book is written in a way that invites the reader to be as courageous as the author has chosen to be. I found her honesty and openness deeply moving. The metaphors throughout the book create vivid images in one's mind, which serve to express complex ideas in a simple, yet powerful and memorable way.

The content is presented in varied and creative ways, such as connecting the Notice, Name, Pause, Choose Otherwise model to a poem; bringing the ancient Four Noble Truths of Buddhism into the subject of trauma healing; or bringing mindfulness to one's Buddhist personality type as a means of self-discovery.

Each mention of a practical application leads the reader down the road of greater self-compassion and reduced self-judgment."
—Rev. Dr. Lori A. Parker, SEP, GCFP, founder of the Embodied Mindfulness Method

"Pawan Bareja's *Reignite Your Power* is a fresh and useful guide for moving yourself or helping others move beyond having trauma define and limit their life. She offers an integrated plan for building resilience through mindfulness and numerous practical resources for self-empowerment. She has such clarity in her descriptions that all the offerings are understandable and seem doable. It is both very useful and a good read."
—Phillip Moffitt, author of *Dancing with Life, Awakening Through the Nine Bodies* and *Emotional Chaos to Clarity*.

"*Reignite Your Power* is a profound yet practical guide to understanding ourselves with greater compassion. Pawan speaks to a global audience with such wisdom and inclusivity that it will leave you feeling seen and connected within this shared web of humanity. Her mindfulness exercises are gentle and accessible—even for beginners. My life has changed for the better because of this book."
—Jillian Abby, craniosacral therapy practitioner, author of *Perfectly Queer: Facing Big Fears, Living Hard Truths, and Loving Myself Fully Out of the Closet*

"Dr. Bareja brings the tremendous depth of her spiritual practice and healing experiences within the broad landscape of trauma to contribute multiple perspectives, techniques, skills, and understandings toward living into and through what often seems insurmountable."
—Larry Yang, author of *Awakening Together: The Spiritual Practice of Inclusivity and Community*

"Pawan Bareja makes the daunting nature of trauma understandable and recovery both possible and accessible. Her book cultivates hope and encouragement, gently guiding you through easy-to-follow exercises that help you embody your personal healing first-aid kit and beyond. Pawan's tested tools and techniques shine a light at the end of the trauma tunnel and empower you to walk toward it at your own pace.

With gentleness, tenderness, and unwavering care, Pawan holds you and believes deeply in your ability to heal. The strength of her belief in you bolsters your resolve and encourages you to take the meaningful steps beautifully outlined in this healing guide. Whether your trauma feels large or small, Pawan offers a variety of tools tailored to your unique needs and preferences—ensuring there is something for everyone on the path to recovery."

—Nil Demircubuk, author of *Down to Earth: Demystify Intuition to Upgrade Your Life*

"A remarkable gift, this book is like a wise and patient friend on the journey of healing. With memorable stories, insightful metaphors, and clear teachings, Pawan Bareja offers a detailed road map for transformation—unlocking the hidden power of trauma with mindfulness and love."

—Oren Jay Sofer, author of *Say What You Mean: A Mindful Approach to Nonviolent Communication* and *Your Heart Was Made for This: Contemplative Practices for Meeting a World in Crisis with Courage, Integrity, and Love*

Reignite Your Power

REIGNITE YOUR POWER

RESOLVING TRAUMA THROUGH MINDFULNESS

Pawan Bareja PhD

SHIVANSH HEALING PRESS
SEDONA, ARIZONA

Shivansh Healing Press, Sedona, AZ

Library Congress Control Number: 2025922150
Paperback ISBN: 979-8-9930435-0-0
eBook ISBN: 979-8-9930435-1-7
Book cover and interior design by Christina Thiele
Editorial production by KN Literary Arts

This book is dedicated to Shiva, my beloved, UmaMa, Ganapati, Pervin, Nil, Jodi, Lori, Haresh, and Omji.

To all my students and clients, who have inspired me by healing their trauma and building resiliency using the practices shared in this book.

I dedicate this book to you, my dear reader, and to your inner unfolding.

Contents

DISCLAIMER

The strategies and advice presented in this book are meant to support you in your journey of resolving your trauma and building resilience. They are not a substitute for professional counseling or therapy. Having the guidance of a qualified professionals for personalized support is essential for some people who have experienced complex trauma. In case you have a physical condition that requires special attention, the reader is advised to consult with a professional before doing any of the physical practices suggested in this book, such as breathwork or movement. Where necessary, please find appropriate support for your healing process outside of this book.

Foreword

It was twenty years ago, but I still remember meeting Pawan Bareja when she arrived as a student for a trauma training course in Los Angeles. I was quite struck by her sincerity and deep determination to heal herself. There was something different about Pawan and the way she was so seriously focused on understanding healing. I noticed it in the way she carried herself, the curious questions she asked during my teaching, and the energy she brought to the class space. On several occasions, I recall observing her as she worked with other students in the therapist role. It was then that I witnessed Pawan's innate gifts to bring much healing to many people.

We've stayed in contact since those early classroom days, and I have continued to watch her grow and flourish in her ability to positively impact the lives and healing of others. That is why I was delighted when she asked me to write the foreword for this book, which is a tangible example of her profound work in healing herself and in being of service to multitudes in need of healing in our traumatized world. What struck me most about *Reignite Your Power* was Pawan's unique ability to address the complexities of trauma and trauma resolution using simple and accessible language. She takes the lessons and teachings of Buddhism and makes them come alive with her client and personal stories. To the large group of mindfulness practitioners of one practice or another all over the world, the book offers a clear and basic understanding of trauma and the body that can help practitioners of all mindfulness practices be more trauma informed.

Mindfulness is Eastern psychology's valuable contribution to Western psychology in general, and trauma therapy in particular. Pawan's writings go beyond the introductory tools of mindfulness in offering all those interested in practical ways of bringing in time-tested concepts and techniques from Eastern psychology. In this text she seamlessly incorporates Buddhist psychology to help facilitate psychological healing in oneself and others. Through incorporating the Buddhist personality types in a unique way, Pawan invites readers to more clearly identify their patterns, both the healthy and unhealthy ones. The personality types further inform and deepen the heart-centered practices of loving-kindness, compassion, and forgiveness by providing extraordinarily valuable insights for those looking to live a more whole and fulfilling existence. Love, kindness, compassion, and forgiveness are not only the end results of trauma resolution. We need to cultivate them as resources for trauma healing and imprint them when trauma is resolved. *Reignite Your Power* offers these lovely possibilities.

Even seasoned practitioners of mindfulness will find Pawan's information helpful in improving their mindfulness practices. Through stories and science, Pawan shares insights on how trauma can disrupt mindfulness practices as well as valuable knowledge of how mindfulness practices can be employed to heal trauma. Her balanced approach to the subject shows how we can prevent our mindfulness practices from being thwarted by trauma, and how we can help heal that trauma through mindfulness practices. I consider *Reignite Your Power* a must-have resource for all practitioners of mindfulness practices and trauma therapists looking for additional support for their clients.

I have taught trauma resolution for nearly thirty years in two dozen countries across six continents. Of late, I have been exploring in greater depth the role of awareness and different ways of differentiating and working through it—not just with what the East calls our gross body but also our subtle and collective bodies—to make trauma treatment more effective. Pawan's book has arrived at the right time to continue exploring that awareness. *Reignite Your Power* is the refined fruit of a tree matured through extraordinary life and healing experiences and serious study on a rigorous path of self-development. I am positive that it will have much benefit to diverse audiences. I look forward to continuing to learn from it.

Dr. Raja Selvam, PhD, PhD

Licensed clinical psychologist, developer of Integral Somatic Psychology™ (ISP™), a comprehensive approach based on the latest findings in neuroscience on cognition, emotion, and behavior as well as energy concepts from Eastern Psychology.

Author of *The Practice of Embodying Emotions: A Guide for Improving Cognitive, Emotional, and Behavioral Outcomes*

Introduction

What is it you plan to do with your one wild and precious life?

—Mary Oliver

Trauma is a sleeping dragon. It's hard to comprehend both its incredible power to destroy in one unexpected fiery breath, and its ability to guard, protect, or take flight. Facing this dragon may leave us feeling scared or powerless. It restricts our choices, keeping us frozen in place, unable to experience our full potential as human beings. Its presence seems to rob us of a life filled with love, joy, compassion, awe, and wonder. In Buddhism, dragons, often referred to as *Nāgas*, are powerful symbols of wisdom, strength, and the ability to transcend the ordinary to move into enlightenment. Even still, so many of us hide this trauma dragon. We cover it with a rug, hoping that we won't ever lock eyes with it. But that is not how a dragon is tamed.

At some point, likely when you least expect it, the dragon's spiked tail might swing out and knock your legs out from under you. When you have your back to it, trying to pretend it's not there, you can still feel its hot breath on your neck. You may think that you have the dragon in your power because you've obscured it from people in your everyday life, but you cannot shake off the feeling that it is always there. It may feel like it has robbed you of your power. I've been there.

Since the age of six, I have been a student of meditation and mindfulness. I grew up in a home with deeply spiritual parents: a mother who would pray every day (and sometimes throughout the night) and would fast two to three times per week, and a father who could get so deep into meditation that he would become completely unaware of the conversation his two daughters and wife were having right next to him. This spiritual lineage extended further up my family tree, with my paternal grandmother building several temples and my maternal grandmother devoting each day to reading sacred texts. From a very young age, I was witness to the importance of developing a connection with both our inner and outer worlds.

Even with this knowledge, life threw its challenges my way. There was the tragic passing of my father when I was only a teenager. And my struggles as a foreign student obtaining my PhD in economics in the U.S. Not to mention my life-altering cancer diagnosis at the young age of forty-two, along with many heartbreaking events in between. I realized that meditation and mindfulness were not shields that could prevent harm from happening in my life, but they were the tools that could help me to endure, survive, and once again thrive.

By my mid-thirties, my life seemed like it was all coming together: I had found a professional role that I loved with a wonderful boss and coworkers, my practice of guiding others through trauma healing was thriving, and I was in a loving relationship. This was when I received my cancer diagnosis. For the many of us who have had our lives impacted by cancer, whether directly or through a close family member or friend who was diagnosed, we know that the journey is a true struggle that most often upends our life completely. The toll is physical, mental, emotional, and spiritual. I was forced to put my career on hold. I struggled to make sense of the why and how of my cancer because it did not run in my family. I tried to ignore the cancer and avoid treatment until friends and family, separated by oceans and continents, begged me to please fight it. Some of the relationships I thought were the most solid seemed to disappear almost overnight, and other relationships developed in the most surprising and unexpected places. It was the crumbling of my life as I knew it.

Cancer was a complex trauma that wove the threads of all my previous losses and heartbreaks, whether unprocessed grief of loss of my father as a teenager or other childhood traumas. The thread from the cloth was unraveled and the entire tapestry came loose. I came to call this time the Year of the Butterfly in my journal. It was my transformation into embodied spirituality for healing. If I had just stayed with my spiritual meditation practice, I would have missed addressing the nervous system trauma response in my physical body. I learned to expand my practice, to experience being present with the unpleasant, and to tune in to the energy of my heart. My heart had to learn to open up to receiving care.

Kindness and love touched me deeply during this time because my heart was wide open, vulnerable, and undefended. The love I received was both deeply moving and very difficult to take in. I felt undeserving, unworthy, and weak. I felt confused about why my friends and family loved me so deeply. I am still moved to tears when I think of that time. Staying soft and open-hearted was new for me. I was experiencing the daily singe from my trauma dragon as it inflicted wounds in so many ways, while also feeling a range of profound emotions. Some days I wanted to give up and give in to the trauma, to let the dragon win and be done with the struggle. But then other days I would realize that I was not ready to be done and would say to the dragon, "I'm taking back what is mine."

It is often in this energy that we start to envision what our life could be like if we no longer had to hide from or endure our dragon. We desire a new path forward, even if we have absolutely no idea what that pathway is or how we'll get there. I will tell you that knowing that path exists is enough of a start. We begin the journey of healing, which is an act of courage. The process of healing means that we are ready to acknowledge our trauma for what it is. We are willing to come face to face with our trauma dragon so that we can learn how it works, what it fears, what provokes it, and what calms it. When we can see things for what they are, sit with them, and know them, we open ourselves up to new ways of being.

My cancer journey brought me face to face with my own mortality and beliefs about death. I had painful, adverse reactions to my medication and also a profound gratitude for the Western medical treatment that was keeping me alive. I used meditation, mindfulness, and breathwork to endure the treatments and energize myself to continue working on projects that brought my heart joy and fulfillment. My spiritual practice deepened. I talked to the cells in my body, sending them love and compassion. I was facing my dragon and feeling deeply at peace.

I am a living, breathing, laughing, dancing example of what spiritually embodied mindfulness can do for trauma. Mindfulness practices, in their remarkable simplicity, can have profound effects on our ability to face trauma, metabolize it in our bodies, and come out in a better state than when we started.

While our specific trauma is uniquely ours, there is an incredible interconnectedness to be found in using some of the same tools used by Nelson Mandela, Jack Kornfield, Peter Levine, Joe Dispenza, Oprah Winfrey, Holocaust survivors, mothers in labor, abolitionists, Indigenous cultures protecting their lands, protestors working for freedom, and so many more. As all of them opened up to their trauma, they were able to unearth post-traumatic growth opportunities hidden within them. Mindfulness means reconnecting with our own inner resources of strength, peace, and aliveness, which will enable us to face personal, global, and environmental stressors with a balanced and grounded mind and heart. We become our own best friend and in turn become more present for our friends, family, and community with a greater sense of connection, ease, and belonging.

How to Read this Book

By picking up this book, I want to acknowledge and celebrate you for your courage, because it's a sign that you are willing to take your own healing in your hands and you are ready to work with your own self. This book is a practical guide to support you through mindfulness practices that will help you release trauma, build resiliency, and empower you to move forward in fulfilling your life purpose. The book is interspersed with suggested Mindfulness Tools and examples of students and clients who have used practices in this book to successfully work through their trauma. While their identifying details may have been modified to protect their identities, the heart of their stories remain the same.

Though this book is written with love, care, and gentleness so as not to trigger you, sometimes, it may bring up feelings of heaviness within you. If you are looking at your trauma dragon, especially if it's your first time, the desire to turn away may seem overwhelming. Be gentle with yourself. This is not a book to binge-read or devour in a week or even a month. Nobody is rushing you to do your inner work. There is no deadline, no book club, and no check-in that will force you to move through it. The tools are there for you when you are ready for them. I suggest that you please move forward at your own rhythm and at your own pace. If you are in a particularly tender state at this moment, I recommend starting with part three, which walks you through heart practices, and spending time there supporting your heart before moving into the trauma work in parts one and two.

While teaching, I like to use the analogy of a lotus blooming in mud. When we are in a state of stress, worry, and trauma, it feels like we are stuck in mud. It feels heavy and hard to move out of. As you read this book and work through the exercises, you'll be able to rise like a lotus out of whatever mud has you feeling held down. The beautiful thing is that for a lotus to blossom, it actually needs the mud. The mud offers nutrients to the flower. Similarly, your stress, worries, and trauma are the ground from which your innate happiness and freedom will arise. As you read this book, I want you to stop often to ask yourself: *Am I in the energy of the lotus or mud? Am I making choices in my life that move me toward becoming the lotus or staying in the mud?* I have included an image of a lotus throughout this book to remind you of the lotus within you that blooms within mud while remaining unblemished by mud. You have the capacity to free yourself from the worries, stress, and trauma and live a life that is full of love, kindness, care, joy, and happiness.

Do not be surprised if your feelings and pace change as you move through this book. You might find this journey to feel like smooth sailing at the start. If you discover that your nervous system is in a fight, flight, or freeze state and you are able to shift the trauma response through the Mindfulness Tools, you will enter into a new nervous system state that feels good and may not be as familiar to you. I have found with some clients that when they have a major breakthrough and come out of being stuck in a traumatic response, their brains immediately want to propel them into more rapid healing. The brain begins to fixate on the challenge, asking, "How do we fix this? How do we fix this!"

Most often my response is, "Do *less!*" Trauma resolution is not a race to be won, but a practice to be honored daily. I make no claims that there will be complete healing, where your trauma will somehow disappear from your mind, body, and emotions. What I do hope you'll find, however, is that the symptoms of your trauma will decrease over time in frequency and intensity. Your whole relationship to the trauma changes as the life force bound up by trauma is opened and released. I want you to be prepared for the immense energy that gets freed up, which you can use for your dream projects, living your life purpose, or serving others. This immense energy is the power within you that is covered by the trauma dragon. As you reignite your power, the dragon energy transmutes into greater aliveness.

Setting Appropriate Expectations

My dear teacher, friend, and mentor, Jack Kornfield, is a sought-after leader in the field of trauma and mindfulness. After enduring horrifying traumas in his youth, Jack—to this day—handles his trauma with extreme care and thoughtfulness. He always begins by doing something that feels good or calming to his nervous system, like sharing a joyful moment from his day. Then he will address a small slice of his traumatic past—a morsel to be digested slowly. Then Jack returns his nervous system to a relaxed and regulated state. Jack has been an inspiring example to remind me that trauma has no timeline and that one of the best things we can do is honor our own needs in the process. We don't heal *from* trauma; we heal *with* trauma. We don't erase our past. We recognize the role it has played in creating who we are and who we desire to be.

One of the most unexpected things I've discovered in my years of working with trauma is that once people truly understand trauma, they can learn the skills to work with it. Trauma is in your roots. It may be part of the soil you grew in. You cannot change the soil you were planted in, but you have a choice to change your inner garden with the nervous system practices offered in the Mindfulness Tools throughout this book. You can plant new seeds of mindfulness practices that grow your love, kindness, joy, equanimity, and gratitude so that forgiveness naturally releases your heart and you can let go of old wounds. And you can begin to cultivate a community with those who care and show compassion and kindness to you, shield you from life's storms, and can help you grow into the most magnificent and fruitful version of yourself.

But this takes time. Patience. And so much love.

My wish for you is that you recognize and reignite your power, that you gain courage in your heart, and that you feel zest and aliveness in your life. I am so grateful to be part of your life-changing journey.

PART ONE

Understanding Trauma
and Mindfulness

Our Relationship with Trauma

What if all of us are one question away from the next big breakthrough in our lives?

—Joe Dispenza

Peacocks are fascinating creatures. I've found myself drawn to them for many years without knowing why. Perhaps it's because peafowl are native to India, my country of origin. But that didn't feel like enough to explain why I felt such a connection to them. There had to be something deeper.

One day I was taking a class on mindfulness and Tibetan Buddhist philosophy, when the teacher brought up the symbolism of the peacock. I was delighted that the answer I had been seeking had found me. The teacher shared that peacocks have the remarkable ability to ingest certain venomous snakes, and as a result, build immunity to them.[1] There was a belief in Tibetan Buddhist tradition that their vibrant plumage, what they are most well-known for, assisted in transmuting the toxins into something safe.[2] These feathers have been used in Traditional Chinese Medicine and Ayurveda for healing for centuries, and there is even scientific research to support this.[3]

What a metaphor for life! We are all faced with trauma at various times in our lives. What we do with that trauma, whether we choose to work with it or avoid it completely, has a lasting impact on our lives. Trauma, like poison, can be our undoing. The peacock, however, teaches us that that is not our only option. Like this resplendent bird, it is possible to transform our trauma, heal from it, and grow more resilient. Working through our trauma may create some of the most incredible, beautiful, and inspiring aspects of who we are and how we show up for others. Over time, you will be able to transmute the poison of trauma into the inner beauty of love, kindness, and joy.

I would be remiss if I painted a picture that makes trauma healing look easy. We cannot simply digest the trauma and suddenly have a perfect life. The journey to healing trauma and building resilience is a continual, lifelong practice. It is layered and nuanced, with each person needing different techniques at different times. It is often a road of many small celebrations and breakthroughs, rather than one pivotal moment of healing.

Throughout this book I have been gifted permission to share many client stories and exercises with you. Some will resonate more than others, depending on where you are in your healing. Some may feel better to you than others. Healing trauma starts with taking small steps. It reminds me of my student, Marie.

Marie wobbled and then grabbed for her chair. Her heart was beating at a rate that would have been abnormally fast for most humans. This had become her new normal. The racing heart was accompanied by dizziness or lightheadedness, which made any physical exertion—even standing—feel like a Herculean feat. Standing for two minutes was about all Marie could bear.

Marie's diagnosis of tachycardia had robbed her of the life she used to know. It was a life where she had been active, out, and involved with the world. She didn't know, nor did her medical team, what brought on this condition. What Marie did know was that she didn't want to continue living this way. She was desperate for answers and anything that might help her reclaim her power over her body and give her a chance of returning to the life she had once known.

Somehow, she happened across a class I was teaching on mindfulness practices for healing trauma. She was at her wits' end and, like many who find me and my work, I was her last resort. With a beginner's mind and an open heart, we started our journey together.

There was nothing miraculous that I was able to offer Marie. In fact, the information, tools, and techniques I am sharing with you in this book are the same ones that I taught her. My mindfulness techniques are not fancy or complicated, but they have persisted through the centuries for the simple fact that they work. Mindfulness has brought healing and relief to people of all cultures, religions, ethnicities, identifications, and abilities around the world. It has helped both the youngest and oldest members of our civilization, the richest and the poorest, the healthiest and the most desperate for health. It may not be the panacea that cures all ills, but for so many it has both improved their quality of life and their transition to death.

By the end of her fourth class with me, Marie was able to remain standing for a remarkable twelve minutes—a 500% improvement in her ability. I was delighted with her progress but also encouraged her to take things slowly and not push herself too fast or too hard. She winked at me, and with a huge grin revealed that twelve minutes wasn't even her maximum time! When she was home and could be in a complete state of calm to practice her mindfulness exercises, her ability to stand was even longer. She was taking back control of her nervous system and reclaiming her life.

The Spiritual Wound of Trauma

In the West, we pathologize trauma, considering ourselves weak and a failure if we fall apart under the intensity of our trauma symptoms. In many cultures, however, trauma is considered a valuable rite of passage. Healers and shamans in such cultures discover their spiritual calling after suffering debilitating wounds, illness, mental afflictions, or diseases like cancer. Trauma is not located just in your emotions, nervous system, or physical body. I've come to realize that it is a spiritual wound—a wound that guides you on your spiritual path as you attempt to unravel the knots of that trauma.

After someone experiences trauma, it's as if they become like the famous Japanese *kintsugi* pottery. In *kintsugi*, a broken piece of pottery is not considered ugly and cast away in the trash. Instead, it is cherished, and the cracks in the pottery are filled with gold. The *kintsugi* pottery is seen as even more beautiful than it was before it broke. The trauma to the pot becomes a rite of passage, leading to the creation of a unique—and stronger—work of art.

I like to give the example of the historical Buddha, Siddhartha Gautama, born around 2,500 years ago. As a prince, he lived a very sheltered life in his palace, surrounded only by beauty, joy, and happiness. He had a lovely wife, whom he got along well with, so he had not seen any pain or suffering in his life. Then one day, he stepped out of the castle, and he saw an old man. He hadn't seen anybody this old and decrepit before, so it was a blow to the heart for him to discover that human bodies age in such a way. The second time he went out of the castle, he saw someone who was extremely sick. He hadn't seen a sick person before, as he had been protected from such realities of life, so again he was very deeply pained by this sight. Finally, he went out and saw a corpse—another deeply depressing experience.

These three events of suddenly seeing someone who was old, somebody who was sick, and somebody who was dead all changed his world view. He was traumatized by seeing this reality of life. But these difficult experiences motivated him to abandon his privileged life as a prince, leave his home, and become a monk. He wanted to find a way to understand the realities of life and to help minimize suffering, even for people facing old age, sickness, and death. How can one move past such suffering? His discoveries as a monk led to him becoming the Buddha, an awakened one, and thus he developed his teachings that have helped many people.

I personally relate to the story I've just shared of the Buddha because when I was treated for cancer in 2007, I used spiritually embodied mindfulness practices to help me get through that time. At the end of the treatment, I felt like I had gone through years of meditation retreats in that one year, and I wanted to share my insights. Of course, I'm not comparing myself to the Buddha or claiming to be enlightened, but just like the Buddha, I wanted to share my newfound knowledge. That's how I started teaching mindfulness, including to young women in their twenties and thirties who had cancer. They started having conversations about trauma, and that's how I found my life passion, just like the Buddha found his after his shock around the realities of old age, sickness, and death. Once he discovered liberation through mindfulness, he taught it for forty years, despite his own health challenges. For me, my journey began in teaching trauma resolution using mindfulness.

I invite you to join me in exploring the transformational possibilities arising out of your own life challenges and your own trauma. Trauma is certainly a curse; it is debilitating and hard. But it can also be a blessing in the way it opens up new avenues for your life. As you release your trauma over time, your own purpose will be clarified to you.

My dear friend, colleague, teacher, and mentor, Raja Selvam, has taught Somatic Experiencing for thirty years. From healing his own traumas, he has helped to bring healing to others all over the world. This included founding Integral Somatic Psychology and leading trauma outreach teams to heal tsunami survivors in India for two years and war survivors in Sri Lanka for three years.

In southern India, where he is from, he went with his teams to villages that were devastated by a tsunami. The fishermen there were terrified to go back into the ocean that had killed people and destroyed their homes. Raja's teams worked with tsunami survivors with trauma symptoms in the fishing villages, offering only one session. They did follow-up surveys with the villagers at six months and a year after the initial treatment and found that a significant number of them continued to remain free of their trauma symptoms. They had released the trauma; the fishermen were able to go back to their livelihood of fishing and the wives no longer had panic attacks when their husbands were out at sea.

So Raja basically transmuted his own trauma into finding a method of healing that works for others too, on many different levels. Just as he accessed his own resiliency by traveling and teaching internationally, he helped the villagers access their resiliency and return to their normal lives.

⚘ Mindfulness Tool: Setting Your Intention

You are reading this because you have the goal of resolving trauma, correct? What are you hoping to gain as a result of working through trauma? If resolving trauma is your goal, then that's your destination. How you treat yourself during your journey is your intention. Let us explore deeper into your intention and carry that intention with you as you continue reading. What is your intention for healing? It may be self-love or self-compassion. Your intention may be to practice better self-care. You may be looking to experience more peace and calm in your life. Identify your intention and practice it with each future section that you read in this book. If your intention is self-love, then as you read future chapters, connect to that feeling and notice your body sensations, thoughts, and emotions as you practice your intention. If you are tired or if your trauma dragon is rearing its head, the practice of self-love in the moment may be to put the book down. Perhaps you need to take a walk in nature or call a friend or do something else that will soothe your mind, heart, and body. Your self-love will change from moment to moment, so I encourage you to check in with yourself often.

The Origins of Trauma

Our ancestors lived in communities and survived as hunter-gatherers. Those of our ancestors who were happy-go-lucky and not aware of their environment were at risk of being attacked by wild animals. If they just sat around daydreaming, they got eaten really fast! The people who survived were the paranoid ones. Those of us alive today are most likely the descendants of our more cautious ancestors, the people who were wary, alertly watching for predator animal tracks and listening for distant sounds of danger. Their genes are in you and me.

This feeling of being overly cautious and looking for danger is called *hypervigilance*. When we are overly cautious, our nervous system does not settle. Even while we are safely nestled in the comfort of our home, even though no tiger is waiting to jump out at us, our nervous system is actively looking for danger.

Brain scientists call this negativity bias. This means that the brain is always on the lookout for the next threat due to the genes we have inherited. It also means that we notice pain more than pleasure and that our negative interactions have a longer-lasting impact on us than our positive ones. So basically, our mind is designed to figure out what is wrong, what's not working, what's broken. It's very natural and just how our minds work.

Our minds aren't paying so much attention to the positive aspects of our life. You know this for yourself. Assuming that your body is functioning normally, then right now your heart is beating and your digestion is moving, the last meal you ate getting absorbed and the nutrition being sent to all the different parts of your body. Everything is ticking along normally and beautifully in your body, so your mind isn't really noticing those things.

But say you suddenly stub your toe or drop something on it and hurt it. You'll have a hard time taking your mind off that sore toe because your mind is geared toward focusing on what's going wrong. The mind gets stuck on the pain because it's hardwired to do so. And once the mind gets stuck on the parts that are not working, it puts all its attention there; it grabs hold of it mentally, and it doesn't let go! Similarly, if there's an emotional insult or injury, the brain does not easily let it go and keeps mulling it over with recursive thinking, making it harder for you to heal, let go, and move on.

If the innate negativity bias of the brain is compounded with trauma, it can lead to our overreaction to any negative information. What I hope to do in this book is help you learn how to release your attention, work with your brain's negativity bias, and let go of some of the trauma symptoms that are weighing you down. My desire is to help you build resiliency so that you are able to take future challenges easily in your stride.

The Spectrum of Trauma

Trauma can result from any life event that overwhelms our ability to take it in stride, although the impact of a painful, fearful, or violent event varies from person to person. Trauma expert Dr. Peter Levine believes that trauma is the body's response to a person's inability to complete their fight, flight, or freeze response in a threatening situation.[4] As a result, immense life force is bound up in the body and results in trauma symptoms.

Not everyone responds in the same manner to a difficult event. For example, two soldiers in the same war may have different responses. One may come home with post-traumatic stress disorder (PTSD) symptoms and the other may not. Similarly, two children in the same abusive household may have different responses to the abuse. One may become an alcoholic and the other a therapist or a CEO of a large corporation. Both are trying to resolve their underlying trauma in different ways.

Here are some common ways of describing different kinds of trauma:

- **Acute trauma** is when you experience a single, time-limited event that traumatizes your nervous system.

- **Chronic trauma** arises through multiple traumatic events over an extended period.

- **Complex trauma** arises from the compounded impact of multiple traumatic events beginning in childhood and continuing into adulthood, resulting in significant impact to emotional regulation, self-perception, and relationship.

- **Secondary trauma**, also called vicarious trauma, arises when you are exposed to others being traumatized. This includes family, friends, partners, or even strangers. Repeated exposure to others being traumatized is even more likely to become traumatizing to the observer unless they are trained in how to cope with it. That's why watching violent movies or war scenes in the news can be particularly disturbing, especially at night. First responders can also suffer from this kind of trauma.

- **Toxic stress** occurs when difficult traumatic experiences lead to prolonged stress in the body that results in fatigue and illness.

- **Compassion fatigue** occurs due to cumulative physical, emotional, and psychological effects of exposure to traumatic stories while working with or helping others with serious illness or trauma. First responders like doctors, nurses, hospice workers, and therapists are exposed to this kind of stress and often start to display traits of compassion fatigue.

- **Childhood situational trauma** occurs when a child's parent or caregiver is incarcerated or is addicted to drugs or alcohol. It also occurs if the child is being bullied or harassed.

Similarly, we experience a spectrum of trauma including birth (our experience as we come out of the birth canal during labor), falling multiple times as we learn to walk, developmental trauma, attachment wounding from neglect or not being seen by parents, bullying in schools, heartbreak from our first love, job loss as a young adult, and so on. These are cumulative traumas. Finally, there can be a straw that breaks the camel's back—a small event that causes our body to exhibit complex symptoms.[5]

Trauma often feels like climbing a ladder of arousal, beginning with the initial response of fight or flight. If you get upset, angry, or rageful in response to the threat, you are in a *fight* response. If you feel anxious, fearful, or terror, your body is in a *flight* response. If trauma is severe or prolonged, you will likely move up the trauma response ladder to a *freeze* state. During a freeze response, you may not feel the body sensations or emotions that others can see in you. For example, a therapist or a teacher may compassionately comment that you are carrying a lot of grief within you, but you may feel your usual self with no grief. A bodyworker or a physical therapist may ask you to drop your shoulder or relax your hips to find relief from your back pain. But you may not feel the tightness in your shoulders or hips. That's due to freeze in that part of the body. It is interesting to note that when someone is healing themselves from a freeze state, they may shift back into feelings of fight or flight and need new techniques to address this different state of nervous system. It's why healing from trauma cannot be generalized. It's why what works for one person may not work for another.

It's important to note that the fawn response (sometimes known as appease) is a recognized trauma response that's more complex. In simplified terms, *fawn* is an automatic and involuntary physiological response to perceived danger and involves nuanced psychological attempts to mitigate the threat. For the sake of discussing the nervous system response, I consider fawn to be out of the scope of this book. I did, however, include some client examples of fawn responses in chapter three, if you'd like to explore more later.

According to a study on adverse childhood experiences (ACEs), if you've had a rough childhood where you experienced physical or emotional abuse or neglect, or if you grew up in a dysfunctional household where there was substance abuse or physical abuse or an incarcerated relative, then you may be at risk of physical health issues due to that childhood trauma. You can find the simple ACEs test on the internet if you want to learn your own score.

On a more positive note, if a person with a high ACEs score from a traumatic childhood has even one loving person in their life—say a grandmother, aunt, uncle, or the parents of a friend—the impact of their trauma is significantly reduced. Social engagement, a theme I will discuss throughout this book, is one of the primary ways that we can heal from trauma. Positive experiences with such loving people are called *resources* and they create a sense of safety, connection, and happiness. These resources act as touchstones or emotional counterbalances when difficult emotions arise.

Robin was a Native American woman who grew up in a household where her father severely abused her mother. The abuse didn't happen in front of the children, but Robin knew what was happening. Ironically, her father loved her and her brother and did not abuse them. He finally separated from Robin's mother and left the family. Robin grew up and was the first one in her family to leave the reservation and find a high-paying job in the medical field. By the time she was in her thirties, she had found a loving partner after a string of abusive relationships.

Five years before I met her, Robin had a small incident while carrying something heavy at work, and it triggered immense pain in her right arm and shoulder. She was unable to type or do almost any kind of work. Logically, there was no reason that the light weight she was carrying should have triggered such a strong response, but it did. To

Robin's bewilderment, regular medical treatments did not heal the pain. Her pain was so intense that Robin finally had to receive disability accommodations at work. The reason Robin could not get better was that she was manifesting symptoms of a childhood trauma that she couldn't remember in detail, and she needed help in finding relief.

Trauma is a physiological process with psychological and emotional repercussions. Robin's childhood trauma led to her nervous system being habitually vigilant to threats in her environment. Even though she was settled with a job and a loving partner, her nervous system was still responding to a raging father who might enter the home without any prior warning. It didn't matter that her adult life environment was safe; her nervous system was still stuck in the past as she felt jumpy and was constantly looking for something to go wrong. She could not pick up the safety signals from the present to drop into a state of relaxation, and she struggled with getting restful sleep for several years. She was easily irritated, frustrated, and stressed if her insurance company did not call her back immediately and often berated the clueless and innocent customer service reps over the phone.

When Robin first started feeling the pain in her arm, how could she have known whether the pain was related to past trauma or an undiagnosed medical condition? The debilitating pain was certainly out of proportion to the weight she had carried at work. When traumatic symptoms show up without an obvious cause, it is difficult to relate them to past trauma.

One way to tell whether you've experienced trauma is by paying attention to your natural response when you find yourself consistently avoiding situations that evoke difficult emotions or memories of an event, or that bring up uncomfortable body sensations. For example, Robin would avoid situations where she felt she did not have much control. Her natural tendency was to avoid childhood-related thoughts or feelings or external reminders of her trauma such as people, places, conversations, activities, objects, or situations.

Some clients who have been in car accidents show avoidance behaviors by choosing to walk everywhere, refusing to drive, or even taking public transportation. With Robin, part of her avoidance was to leave the reservation and build a successful life in the city. The avoidance of childhood traumatic memories empowered her to succeed in her career.

⚜ Mindfulness Tool: Grounding

This is a practice you can do anytime to feel more connected to your body, but as we are discussing trauma, you may be feeling anxiety or tightness rise up in your body. Before you begin, take a moment to ground yourself and let loose of the emotional charge from your body. Once you feel calm and grounded, proceed to the next section.

1. Start by sitting comfortably on a chair. If you can do so, place your feet squarely on the floor and allow your back to rest against the chair.

2. Gently press your feet into the ground for five seconds and release. Do this at least three times, and sense into your body after releasing to see if your breath is deeper or if your feet feel more in touch with the ground.

3. Find a sitting posture where your back is straight and supported by the chair. Now place a palm on your chest and another on your belly. With each breath, feel the rise and fall of your hands.

4. Bring an attitude of gentleness to your self-touch, as if you are holding a good friend or a loved one. Sit with this gentleness toward yourself for a few breaths. Notice after a few moments whether your breath is deeper and if you feel more calm, centered, and grounded.

Identifying and Acknowledging When You've Experienced Trauma

Most of us have experienced challenging emotional or physical episodes in our lives. These can be as seemingly simple as a sports injury or as complex as years of childhood abuse. Severe situations can lead to PTSD. When we are children, and even later as adults, we may not initially register an event as traumatic. Many of the symptoms might take years to appear, and when they do, we might not connect them with any particular experience. Children are especially vulnerable to negative experiences that might appear minor to an adult.

You may have experienced a trauma that created such overwhelming body sensations, emotions, or repeated thought patterns that you used unhealthy coping strategies to numb yourself. People often turn to excessive use of food, drugs, alcohol, and sex. When we are traumatized, our nervous system is affected, so of course we use whatever coping method we can to numb out and avoid painful feelings that arise, such as a generalized feeling of lack of safety, hyper self-criticism, or constantly being riddled by trauma-related emotions such as fear, horror, anger, guilt, or shame. Some people may feel withdrawn, isolated, and alienated, shying away from interaction with loving people and pleasant activities.

We'll talk more about nervous system coping strategies in a later chapter and delve deeper into working with releasing the nuances of trauma in our lives. For now, it's enough to know that trauma affects different layers of the body, mind, and heart, but it always expresses itself through symptoms. It may show up in our memories, dreams, emotions, flashback images, or physical symptoms in the body. The way to know if you've experienced trauma is to notice the symptoms that are coming up.

Generalized Symptoms of Trauma

Symptoms are the language of trauma. To gain a better understanding of your own trauma, circle in pencil the ones you relate to at present. As you read this book and practice the exercises, I suggest that you return to this symptoms list to see if the frequency and intensity of the symptoms have decreased; a sign that you are healing yourself.

Anxiety and panic attacks

Phobias

Depression

Hopelessness

Decreased concentration

Physical or emotional numbness

Loss of interest

Irritability

Self-destructive behavior

Loss of sense of self or identity

Feeling unreal or out of body

Sleep disturbances

Feelings easily hurt

Excessive worrying

Abrupt mood swings

Uncontrollable rage

Problems connecting with others

Being easily startled

Hypervigilance and hyperactivity

Avoidance behaviors

Attraction to danger

Accident proneness

Feeling frozen or immobile

Forgetfulness

Shakiness or dizziness

Constant fear of dying

Hypersensitivity to sound or light

Disruptive thoughts, flashbacks, or nightmares

Headaches and other chronic pain

Digestive problems

Asthma attacks

Neck and back problems

Frozen joints

Chronic fatigue

General and localized pain

Performance problems in sports, sex, or other activities

⟨Ϙ⟩ Mindfulness Tool: Your Resiliency Wheel

In this exercise, we are exploring your strengths that make you resilient in the face of life challenges. When complete, keep your Resiliency Wheel, as we will revisit it when we get to chapter 5.

1. Draw a circle on a sheet of paper and create nine sections in the circle, like nine slices of pie. Write down the names of these core areas of your life in each section:

   - Home/Belonging

   - Work

   - Spirituality

   - Family/Loved Ones

   - Money/Abundance

   - Physical/Emotional/Mental Health

   - Fun/Play/Creativity

   - Friendship/Romance

   - Purpose/Self-Expression

2. Determine how well things are working in each area. Create a subjective Resilience Scale for each area by rating it from 0 to 10 and marking the appropriate area in the pie chart. A rating of 10 means that an area of your life is working perfectly; it is open, relaxed, and joyous! Give the lowest numbers to areas of high stress and difficulty.

3. Write a sentence describing each of these areas of your life, considering what is going well and what isn't working.

4. Mark the areas associated with any difficult events you have experienced, such as heartbreak from a relationship, job loss, or war trauma. Notice if any of these areas coincide with the lower

ratings. Sometimes one or more areas may be challenging due to trauma symptoms.

5. Notice which areas are going well. What are your qualities or strengths that are making these areas go smoothly? These qualities and strengths are your resources.

Mindfulness and Trauma

What seems to be most effective in ending the trauma cycle is the practice of mindfulness. This means bringing mindfulness techniques to the trauma experience in your body and emotions so that healing can be sustained over time.

Mindfulness helps us recognize that trauma is present and that something is going on with us. If we can stay present with it long enough to recognize it, then we can start to investigate what's going on. Mindfulness also puts trauma in perspective; it's just another state of mind. It helps us contain the trauma. Otherwise, we get swept away by the traumatic symptoms and we spin out. Mindfulness brings us to the present moment where there is a space of respite from the trauma. From there, we can engage in activities that are calming and soothing to the heart, mind, and body. In this way, healing can occur sustainably over time.

In the next chapter, we'll talk more about mindfulness, and in chapter three, we'll talk about the nervous system and trauma. We'll explore how mindfulness can help you recognize and effectively work with the cycle of trauma. The most effective way to heal trauma is an integrated approach using mindfulness and body-based practices to work with the nervous system.

For now, let's take a pause and breathe. It is all too easy for even small traumatic experiences to get triggered by reading about trauma! We will go slowly and gently in this book to avoid this happening, but I need you to help by repeatedly taking breaks. Look out of the window, take a walk, or do some small activity around the home as you open deeper into this topic. I want you to build resiliency as you read this book and not re-trigger a stress response in your nervous system.

☸ Mindfulness Tool: Your Relief Resources Inventory

Take some time to create an inventory of all the practices that you are currently doing that are helping you find some relief from your trauma symptoms. What I'm calling practices can be very simple: dancing, exercising, eating foods you enjoy, laughing, spending time with friends, and so on. Taking an inventory of your natural strengths is important so that you can remember to use them when you need to calm your nervous system.

Mindfulness as a Tool for Trauma Healing

Breathing in, I calm body and mind. Breathing out, I smile.
Dwelling in the present moment I know this is the only moment.

—Thich Nhat Hanh

Sat-chit-ananda. It's a Sanskrit phrase and it means "truth-consciousness-bliss." This is our innate nature, our true power, and is the foundation of every person. Whether we realize it or not, our purest form is truth, consciousness, and bliss. Everything else is a layer that life has placed upon us that may distance us from our true nature. Our *sat-chit-ananda* is like the most perfect clear-blue sky.

When I think of trauma and its effects on human beings, I envision it like a thunderstorm that rolls in, bringing darkness and clouding the skies. The rain may pour and the thunder may boom. But regardless of how ominous the storm may be, no matter how long the storm may last, beyond those clouds that perfect blue sky, the *sat-chit-ananda*, still exists. It never goes away, even in the presence of the trauma. It simply becomes harder to see.

How do we access our natural state, particularly when trauma has cast a shadow on our lives? How do we reignite our power? The answer is mindfulness. Mindfulness, in its many forms, can help us move closer to our *sat-chit-ananda*. Mindfulness can bring us in touch with our joy, love, kindness, and experiencing the joy of others. It brings us feelings of equanimity. But, like all wellness techniques, mindfulness is not healing in and of itself. Sitting on the floor in an uncomfortable position for twenty minutes a day while your brain gets annoyed with you will not bring you closer to joy. Instead, it may do the opposite! Mindfulness techniques should be done in a way that moves us toward our true nature so that we feel better from them, not frustrated with them. Mindfulness can also help us become more aware and empathetic when others are not in their true nature. It reminds me of the story of Sonia and Mark.

Sonia was a young woman in her early twenties when she was diagnosed with cancer. She was supported by her boyfriend, Mark, as she endured the difficult chemotherapy and radiation treatments. It was during this time that Sonia found my mindfulness classes. Together we used the many tools of mindfulness to help her work through and resolve traumas, both past and present, until she was in remission.

While this should have been a joyous time to celebrate, during this same time Mark was also diagnosed with cancer. Knowing the level of support and care that it took to help Sonia through her treatments, Mark opted instead to break off their relationship. His rationale was that after all she had been through, he did not want to put her on a new, difficult journey of being his caretaker during treatment. He felt that cancer had already robbed them of time they should have been enjoying each other's company.

The reality was that Sonia wanted to take care of him. She wanted to be there to help him in his time of need and teach him the mindfulness-based trauma resolution exercises she had benefited from so much during her own treatment. Each of us has our own journey, though. I suggested that out of love and compassion for Mark, she not force her experience on him and instead wait for him to express interest. I did not want her to be construed as his stress police. I knew that Mark already had an awareness of these exercises, as he was witness to them during Sonia's treatments. He had to find them when he was ready for the type of healing mindfulness can provide.

Eventually, Mark and Sonia reconnected as friends and (as she'd hoped) he asked her to teach him the mindfulness exercises that had been so instrumental in her own healing. It did not take long for him to experience a similar benefit as he worked through layers of trauma. Like Sonia, Mark eventually reached a state of cancer remission.

This was not the end of mindfulness in their lives, however. Together they began to move through life like stress detectives, using their mindfulness skills to navigate the challenges of daily life. Mindfulness and tuning into their own self-awareness helped them empathically read the state of other people's nervous systems like the store clerk who seemed withdrawn or the aggressive driver on the highway. As such, they were able to respond rather than react to them and keep their own nervous systems well-balanced.

In the face of trauma, an untrained mind will use a coping strategy of either escaping into the past with regret or racing into the future, replaying what-if scenarios. Rather than help, these coping strategies often create additional unhappiness. Mindfulness helps bring you into the present and invites you to recognize that there is something wrong. When you feel the raindrops of the storm, you are better equipped to decide what to do about it. You can begin to work with your trauma and help to contain its symptoms, like anxiety or depression. Mindfulness is not the magic wand that makes the storm disappear and life return to normal, but it does give you visibility into what you're facing so that you can make the best possible decisions for yourself.

Normalizing Trauma with the Noble Truths of Buddhism

Mindfulness is what allowed Sonia and Mark to be present in what they were experiencing, and they can now gift that empathetic presence to others. Their ability to show up for others means that the people in their lives, whether close relationships or casual encounters, may now feel less alone simply due to being seen. One of the most difficult things we can experience in life is that lack of connection or feeling of aloneness. It is inherent in our survival that we stay with the pack, just as a zebra must stay with the herd or else it is placing itself at a greater risk of getting chosen as prey by a lion.

Mindfulness is what I call the *social engagement* of the nervous system. It is what brings us back to our herd and creates a feeling of safety. This relates strongly to the first of the Four Noble Truths of Buddhism. The Four Noble Truths are traditionally identified as the first teachings of the Buddha and the most important teachings in Buddhism for their liberating insight. They are the understanding of suffering and also the guide to overcoming it.

The First Noble Truth

The First Noble Truth is the truth of suffering. The shared human experience of suffering shows up in all forms of stress, anxiety, worry, unhappiness, and unsatisfactoriness. It demonstrates that the little and large traumas of life are common to all human beings. In the metaphor of trauma being a thunderstorm, the First Noble Truth helps us to realize that these thunderstorms are not just raining on us alone. In this world of more than eight billion people, there are hundreds, thousands, or millions of others who have been through the same thing.

When we are experiencing trauma, having an awareness of the First Noble Truth is helpful in that it limits our ability to be isolated or victimized. We are never alone in our experiences, even if we have yet to meet the people who have gone through the same. It is moving out of this isolationist mindset that is so important to growing beyond the pain of trauma. Our most elderly and most sick members of our society are the two groups at a greater risk of harm from social isolation. Mindfulness techniques that reconnect them (even if in their own minds) to society can be incredibly helpful to these struggling populations. It brings them back to the herd.

The Second Noble Truth

The Second Noble Truth is that our suffering is caused by clinging. Trauma becomes like being stuck in an eddy or whirlpool, our world swirling around us and keeping us stuck in the same dangerous spot. Have you felt that swirling before? Thoughts or memories replaying that you just can't seem to break free of? The mind, specifically the amygdala, tends to wrap itself around difficult events and does not let the event or the feelings go.

The amygdala is a small, almond-shaped structure in our brains that is part of the limbic system—the network that controls moods and emotions, motivation or drive, and instincts. It has served as an important aspect of our survival, often alerting us to danger and retaining behaviors that keep us safe. The amygdala is also a major fear center that can startle us or send our bodies into panic in the event of real danger or perceived threats. It is often the first area of the brain to be activated when we experience trauma. Both fortunately and unfortunately, our amygdala works very hard to protect us and try to keep us safe. Sometimes, like with trauma recovery, it can work to our detriment and keep us in fight, flight, or freeze in situations where we don't need to be.

What helps the amygdala regulate itself so that we can shift our nervous systems back to homeostasis? Mindfulness, of course! A study published by the National Institute of Health titled "Impact of short- and long-term mindfulness meditation training on amygdala reactivity to emotional stimuli" found that meditation training may take the edge off emotional reactions through reduced amygdala reactivity. The study found that Mindfulness-Based Stress Reduction (MBSR) can have a beneficial effect on our emotion regulation ability.[6] To simplify, mindfulness can truly produce calming effects on our minds and nervous systems. It is scientifically proven.

Can mindfulness help if you don't know what trauma it is that you're holding on to? Absolutely. It reminds me of my client, Laila. Here is her story:

———————

Laila was a Zen student who had a deep meditation practice. She lived at the Zen center and followed their daily practices of meditation combined with communal living and eating. One day, Laila met her teacher for what should have been a quick check-in on her meditation practice. Instead, she found herself crying uncontrollably. It took her almost thirty minutes to calm herself enough to speak. Laila shared that she had no idea what this grief was, nor why it was coming up now. Nothing had changed in her life and, if anything, she was taking steps to live a healthy and wholesome life. To her, it didn't make any sense.

That is when Laila's teacher referred her to me for a deeper exploration. It was natural that Laila wanted to know the "why" behind her recent bouts of uncontrolled sobbing. They seemed to come out of nowhere and did not seem to bring up old memories or sensations. She did not look the least bit pleased when I informed her that the "why" didn't matter at this point. We had to be in the "what."

I shared with her the Buddhist story of the second arrow. In the story, a man is shot by an arrow and will surely die if he doesn't get medical attention soon. As people try to help him, he tells them to stop. First, he wants to understand who shot the arrow. He wants to know why they shot him. He is curious how far away they shot from and what the arrow is made out of. The people plead with him to get help, but he is caught up in his own analysis.

This overthinking is known as the second arrow. It's the second arrow that is really what might kill the man. These seemingly pertinent yet irrelevant questions represent the man shooting himself. If the first arrow doesn't kill him, he will surely die from the second arrow because the second arrow prevents him from working on the primary wound.

The story resonated with Laila and made her realize that the treatment of her trauma would be the same, regardless of the "why" behind it. It took her time to understand that not knowing the reason for her tears was okay. It may have been an event from her distant past or even when she was pre-verbal as a baby or in utero. What helped her in her healing process was to be nonjudgmental and compassionate toward herself when her mysterious grief arose. Then she was able to directly work with the emotion and body sensations and soon the storm of grief passed.

As in Laila's story, attending to the primary trauma symptoms is essential for our trauma resolution journey. Be mindful of the second arrow and set it aside while you tend to the primary trauma and its somatic expression. It is an essential skill in building resiliency. Mindfulness avoids the danger of the second arrow by using what is known as a *bottom-up approach* to healing. It starts with the most basic sensations in the body, bringing us into the present and allowing us to tune in to what we are feeling, tasting, hearing, seeing, smelling, and sensing. Once we have settled, then we move to images that may or may not be present. We settle again and, from there, we move up to the next level, which is our behaviors. The last stage is where we try to apply meaning or the "why" behind the trauma. In each stage we must settle ourselves before moving on to the next stage. The settling is what creates a container for our trauma and keeps it from spiraling out of control.

This bottom-up approach is rooted in the four foundations of mindfulness:

1. Work with the body, in the body.
2. Work with the pleasant, unpleasant, and neutral experiences of life. I refer to these in part two of this book as *flavors of experiences*.

3. Work with the mental formation. This includes emotions like anger and regressive thinking.

4. Work with consciousness.

In consciousness, we become aware that we are everything and everyone. Vietnamese Zen Buddhist monk Thich Nhat Hanh wrote a powerful poem titled "Please Call Me by My True Names"[7] to illustrate this point. In it he identifies that he is both the mayfly and the bird that eats it, the starving child and the arms dealer contributing to the starvation, the rape victim and the rapist. The poem ends with, "Please call me by my true names, so I can wake up, and so the door of my heart can be left open, the door of compassion."

While the full comprehension of the poem may be hard to grasp, the overarching concept is this: We are full of all of the seeds of humanity. Some are seeds of love. Some are seeds of anger. Some of delusion. Some of generosity. The seeds we pay the most attention to with our minds and actions are the ones we are watering. But just as when we water plants, watering the seeds inside of us will inevitably result in watering some weeds as well. This is why we can't expect to be completely free from anger, sadness, hatred, or despair. They are still a part of us. However, we can use mindfulness as a tool to regularly weed our garden and keep their growth in check. In the human experience, it's important that we do not let the weeds take over. We must not cling to them by leaning into our true nature of *sat-chit-ananda*. This is the Second Noble Truth.

The Third Noble Truth

The Third Noble Truth says that healing is *nirodha*—Sanskrit for "cessation." It is the end of suffering and the response to the first two Noble Truths. It essentially says that when we identify that suffering is a part of life and we are willing to release it, we have the ability to heal.

This healing results from making choices and consciously choosing to move toward happiness. It may mean we are choosing to be open or let go or retreat or even forgive. It may mean changing our behaviors and patterns by moving toward things that bring us closer to happiness (like mindfulness) instead of things that take us further away (like doom-scrolling social media). This is where a process that my dear friend, trauma healer, and teacher, Lori Parker, shared in her development trauma class many years ago.

Notice, Name, Pause, Choose Otherwise (NNPCO) is a process I love because it's another way to break down the bottom-up approach to mindfulness. In breaking down the process, we can identify and free ourselves from that which we are clinging to.

- **Notice**: This is the process of identifying a pain, whether old or new. It could be a friend who betrays you, the loss of a family member or your home, a health condition that changes the function of your body, or any number of other things. In this step, we acknowledge its existence.

- **Name**: Describe what you're feeling by calling it something specific. Rather than trying to move past uncomfortable physical sensations like chest pain or dizziness, or emotions like anger or sadness, we acknowledge them.

- **Pause**: When the body, mind, or heart is overwhelmed, it's helpful to Pause and allow our nervous system to process the body's sensations, emotions, and thoughts. This is not a time to take any action or try to force yourself to move on. It is not just passively accepting that we cannot change the past. By allowing ourselves to Pause, we are actually taking the first step in consciously moving toward our happiness and our freedom.

- **Choose Otherwise**: Whether a major step or the smallest movement, this is when we start making new decisions that align us with our path toward happiness. A happy person is not someone with no problems or issues in their life. A happy person is someone who is consciously choosing calmness, joy, love, and happiness. We have a choice in every situation and that is the greatest potential within us.

I like to explain NNPCO with the poem "There's a Hole in My Sidewalk" by Portia Nelson. In the poem, Portia walks near her home and falls into this hole in the sidewalk. This happens several times before she takes the time to Notice that there is a hole there. She stops blaming the sidewalk and begins to Name her lack of judgment in choosing to walk on the same sidewalk. Though she doesn't say it in the poem, let us assume that she Paused and stopped walking on that street for some time. Finally, she Chooses Otherwise by walking around the hole. As she has more freedom, she chooses to walk on another street and avoid the hole completely.

The Fourth Noble Truth

There is a Fourth Noble Truth, which is the Eightfold Path of living in harmony with nature. This core Buddhist teaching starts by understanding the nature of things and avoiding thoughts, words, and actions that harm others and ourselves. This includes the way you earn your living, making a concerted effort to cultivate positive states of mind, and practicing mindfulness and concentration meditation. For the intention of this book, we will not be exploring the topic, but I wanted you to be aware of its existence in case you choose to deepen your practice.

Mindfulness Is the Way to Healing

It's been said that there are two ways to heal trauma: we can change the world we live in, or we can change our internal world. Changing the world we live in is possible to an extent. We can change our geography, how we live, and who we surround ourselves with. However, there are still many factors that are outside our control. We have much greater influence on our internal world, which we have the ability to change through mindfulness and somatic emotional work of releasing trauma stored in our body.

We too can start the work of internal healing through the simplest of exercises. One Minute Mindfulness, the tool that follows, is one I use multiple times throughout the day. It is simple and can be done virtually anywhere no matter what you're doing: sitting, standing, lying down, walking, and so on. One Minute Mindfulness takes us to the first two principles of NNPCO: Notice and Name. It is helpful to break us out of patterns when we find ourselves swirling in the whirlpool of emotion or ruminating over a negative thought. Let's take a moment now to practice this exercise.

☸ Mindfulness Tool: One Minute Mindfulness

Begin by finding a timer or clock to track one minute. You'd be surprised at how long a minute may feel when doing this exercise, so it's helpful to have an external tool to validate the time. Next, we'll bring our awareness to our senses in the present moment. I find it helpful to speak what I'm sensing aloud, if possible.

Some questions to ask yourself as you start this exercise:

1. What is the dominant sensation you're noticing at this moment? It may be something like, *My toes are cold* or *I have an itching sensation on the back of my neck.* Or perhaps it has to do with something you're seeing, smelling, or hearing. *I see the sunlight streaming in through my window. I smell sweet banana bread. I hear a car driving past my house and children playing in the next room.*

2. Check in with your other senses. What do you feel? What do you see? What do you hear? What do you smell? What do you like? What do you sense?

3. Notice any changes in your body. Do you feel any muscles relaxing? Has your breathing changed? You might say something like, *I feel my right shoulder relaxing* or *My hands dropped more loosely into my lap.*

Notice how you feel at the end of one minute compared to the beginning of the exercise. Chances are you may feel more present and aware in the moment. You might feel calmer in your mind, or your body might feel more rooted to the earth. Know that you can return to this exercise whenever you need throughout the day. It is a way to exercise your ability to Notice.

ꕥ Mindfulness Tool: Practicing NNPCO

I believe that the NNPCO framework can be used on almost any kind of situation, whether with yourself or with other people. I suggest trying it out on small moments and practicing it whenever possible with a goal of being able to seamlessly incorporate it whenever challenges arise.

Using what you noticed in the previous exercise, now let us practice using your observations in the NNPCO framework. The following process allows you to practice Noticing what you're experiencing in the present, Naming it, Pausing, and Choosing to transmute your response into a new perspective or decision.

1. Think of a situation you can practice with, such as a difficult conversation you recently had with a beloved, boss, or someone else. For example, you could practice with a situation where you

confronted your roommate or your partner about leaving dishes in the sink.

2. Notice: How did you respond to the situation? What feelings and thoughts arose in you when you saw the dirty dishes? What behaviors did you engage in? In our example, maybe when you saw the dirty dishes in the sink, you thought *I can't believe they did this again after I asked them to just load the dishwasher. It's not that hard!!* Notice the rising tide of emotions within you like irritation, frustration, and anger. And these emotions culminate in you taking the action of yelling at your partner.

3. Name: Write down or say out loud everything that comes up. Name your emotions as *irritation, frustration, anger. Say out loud that you let loose of your anger and yelled at your partner which in turn started an argument. Maybe your breathing is short and quick. Observe you're in a fight response.*

4. Pause: In the midst of feeling anger and frustration, it isn't easy to stop yourself and take a pause. But instead of stomping out of the room, you may consider taking a break for a few moments by practicing One Minute Mindfulness, taking a walk, splashing cold water on your face, or doing something that engages your mind in a different way. If your breathing hasn't returned to normal after your Pause, then I suggest taking a longer pause until you feel settled.

5. Choose Otherwise: Now, come back and look at what you journaled. Can you Choose a new thought pattern and emotion that will bring more happiness, peace, and joy in your life? What new behavior arises out of this new thought pattern and emotion? In our example, can you give your partner the benefit of the doubt that they are not deliberately trying to irritate you? Maybe they are having a stressful day and genuinely forgot to load the dishwasher. A potential new behavior could be that you brainstorm

solutions with your partner that might work for both of you and maintain harmony in your household.

Write down your new response, and spend time rehearsing this new pattern of thought, emotion, and behavior for that situation. It's as if you are getting a chance to replay life and practice this new way of being. Over time, the new thought pattern, and the behavior you've associated with it, will come naturally to you. If it is helpful, talk with a therapist or compassionate friends to identify alternative behaviors.

Why is this step necessary? Sadhguru, an Indian teacher, says, "Every thought, every reverberation you create on the level of the mind changes the chemistry in your body." To create new chemical or hormonal patterns in your body, we need a different set of thoughts.

Perhaps you could reconsider a different situation that went poorly and journal about how you could have followed NNPCO to a new conclusion. This will give you more practice with NNPCO and will enable you to catch yourself earlier in the midst of a triggering situation and tame your stress response.

How Mindfulness Works

There is what feels like both a blessing and a curse to mindfulness. You feel *everything*. Sensations that you may have dissociated from or ignored in the past to "get through the day" suddenly become like a red light that needs to be acknowledged before you can move forward. This initial experience of feeling everything can be frustrating to new mindfulness practitioners hoping to feel better and not worse from the exercises.

Mindfulness means finally acknowledging that trauma is present. It is gifting yourself the permission to notice it, to name it, and to pause in the existence of how it feels. You become your own truth detective, recognizing and investigating your feelings. Be kind to yourself. The ability to feel everything will eventually present itself as a gift, and you will feel like you are living fully, rather than simply going through life.

Mindfulness creates a container in which we can hold our trauma. It may stop the seemingly endless spinning of our minds or the recurring cycles of pain in our physical bodies. Creating this container for trauma allows us to look at it as an observer and explore how we can work with our bodies and use other tools to address it. If you cannot contain your trauma, you can't move beyond it. Building a container for trauma reminds me of my client Selma's story.

Selma was in a nearly constant state of fight or flight when I met her. She was experiencing terrible flashes of images that would send her into a state of panic. What frightened her even more was that she had no story to go with the images. They held no meaning or explanation for her, and yet they would send her nervous system into an unbearably heightened state. As with the story of the second arrow, I knew that we didn't need to explore the "why" behind these images. Instead, we needed to set boundaries to create a container for Selma's trauma to exist.

When people think of mindfulness or meditation, they might envision a person sitting on the floor cross-legged with their eyes shut. In an acute trauma state like Selma's, shutting her eyes and not permitting movement would have only exacerbated her feelings. I encouraged her to keep her eyes open during all exercises, meditations, or traumatic imagery moments in order to orient herself to the space she was in.

Selma's fight or flight response meant that her body was telling her to move. I moved her through movement exercises to restore grounding, like the sweeping exercise at the end of this chapter. We focused on Selma's breath, incorporating exercises like Box Breathing, also included at the end of this chapter. I encouraged Selma to hum, sing, and chant to keep her throat open to vocalization. The Sanskrit "Om Mani Padme Hum" is one of my favorite chants to use in these states as I've found it helpful in overcoming obstacles and gaining wisdom by purifying one's body, mind, and speech. The chant invites the unfolding of our lotus heart to arise from the muddy waters of our daily lives with love and compassion.

With time, Selma learned to notice the images as they appeared and shift herself into using mindfulness tools to bring herself out of the traumatic images, rather than allowing herself to be consumed by them. She chose to change her nervous system response, and with time, the frequency and intensity of the images lessened. They no longer controlled her life.

With Selma, our primary focus was to address her fight or flight mode immediately to keep her from ascending the trauma response ladder to the next phase of arousal: freeze. Fight or flight is still a state where we are more flexible. That flexibility is key to bringing us back to a state of social engagement or oneness with our community. Freeze pushes us toward isolation. Social engagement, our ability to feel a connection to others (whether actually in person or just perceiving it), is one of the most powerful tools in healing from traumatic experiences. We cannot hold meaningful conversations when we are in fight or flight. Our brain shuts down to its most essential level to keep us safe. But we cannot achieve that feeling of social engagement if our nervous systems are in a state of disarray.

After we have consciously felt the pain of repeating an unconscious traumatic behavior over and over again, mindfulness empowers us to break the pattern. It allows us to choose new thought patterns, emotions, and behaviors that move us toward happiness. Resiliency is our ability to choose these thought patterns, emotions, and behaviors that make us happy.

Mindfulness and Resiliency

A client came to me one day, upset and on alert. Life was feeling particularly challenging for her as she was faced with a difficult decision. She explained that she had an incredible job opportunity, but it was far away from her current home. She did not want to miss out on this once-in-a-lifetime opportunity. She saw two paths: One was to uproot her husband and children and move them to the new location with her. The other was to follow this new job alone, returning to visit her family when she was able.

I picked up two pens from my desk and held them like a V in front of her, representing each of the paths she had identified. Then I grabbed a third pen. "What option is this?" I asked.

"I don't know," she responded.

"It's another path," I said. "We see it. I have it here in my hand. It exists. As you were telling me your story, you only saw the two pens. The reality is there are more directions and more paths that you may not even know or haven't been introduced to yet."

In order to be resilient, we must approach life with what is known as a *beginner's mind*. In the beginner's mind, everything is a possibility, including options that we may not even see or know to exist. It is a state of believing in infinite possibilities. To be in this state we must approach life while maintaining our innocence. A beginner's mind is not the naive innocence of a child's mind, which believes that highly improbable things have the same likelihood as probable things. Instead, we approach life with an informed innocence. We are aware that being hit by tragedies is a part of the lived experience. Our informed innocence allows us to recognize that we can bounce back from these tragedies and move forward with a sense of curiosity, joy, and wonder. This helps break the cycle of the dysregulated amygdala.

Trauma is often a failure of imagination. When we cannot see the path forward or we do not believe that a path forward exists, we remain in a traumatized state. It's not our fault. As I mentioned in the first chapter, we are wired to have a negativity bias that keeps us focused on the bad things to keep us safe. Mindfulness and informed innocence implore us to seek the good and to open our minds to infinite positive possibilities.

One beautiful example of this is the chapter one story of the people in the fishing village that was hit by a tsunami. They recovered in part thanks to Raja's mindfulness-based trauma healing techniques. Think about after that tsunami hit. What do you think the fishermen and their families envisioned as their path forward? Most certainly, Raja coming to town and sharing trauma healing exercises was not one of their imagined pathways. They couldn't even envision that possibility, but then that new pathway appeared.

Can you think of any instances like that in your own life? When have you been in a situation where you thought your options were either this or that? Maybe you only saw one path forward and then a new option presented itself. This is a reminder to our dysregulated amygdala that many more possibilities exist than we can even envision or plan for. Some people call these miracles, divine timing, or synchronicities. Sometimes, these options were there all along; we just couldn't identify them from within our traumatized state.

The Journey Versus the Goal of Healing

As we move through our healing process, it is important to discern our healing goals from our healing journey. Each has a different but important purpose. In life, our goals may be something out of our control, but our journey is not. Take, for example, my teaching. My goal when I teach (and with this book) is that I share information in a way that you can understand and use in your own life. I want you to be able to recognize the nervous system, both your own and others', so that you can respond rather than react. I have all of this knowledge to impart to you, but I can't control what you understand, retain, and implement. The only thing I can control is my intention. What is my intention? I keep that very clear for myself: my intention is to create a safe and compassionate space for you so that healing can happen. That is my intention that I have some control over.

Take a moment to refer back to the Setting Your Intention Mindfulness Tool you did in chapter one. It is important to keep this reminder with you as you go through your journey. When we are focused on the intention of the journey, rather than the goal, we need to become comfortable with patience in the process. The poet Rainer Maria Rilke once implored a young poet to have patience with everything that is unresolved in their heart. He advised the poet to try to love the questions themselves, as if there were locked rooms or books written in a foreign language. Rilke advised not to spend time searching for answers, which one may not find easily at the moment.

You may be asking questions such as:

- Why did this traumatic event happen to me?
- Why did this person I loved dearly abandon me?
- Why did my family not support me when I was hurting?
- What is the path to healing my trauma?
- How do I let go and forgive this violent act?

Rilke advises that even if these answers were given to you, paradoxically, you would not be able to live them.

The start of our trauma healing journey is filled with confusion and chaos. Rilke says that the point of a healing journey is to live everything, even the chaos and confusion. His advice is to live the questions and experience the journey. We can change the questions for ourselves. Instead of wanting to understand the goal, we can ask about the journey.

- How do I stay present in this moment, and in the next moment?
- How do I become resilient?
- What is the path forward for freedom from this pain in this moment?

Hold your questions and live your questions. Your response to these questions will change from one moment to the next and from one day to the next. Perhaps in the far future, you may realize that you are living the answers to your questions.

☸ Mindfulness Tool: Sweeping Our Body

Sweeping was an effective tool in helping my client Selma move out of fight or flight when she was experiencing troubling images. I suggest you do this in the morning and evening. Spending five minutes practicing this will help you face the stressors of the day in a more grounded manner with an even and balanced mind.

1. Sit or stand comfortably.
2. Using gentle pressure, move your right palm gently down your left arm, stroking the left arm from your shoulder down to your fingertips. Move slowly so that you can keep your awareness in your palm and be present for your own touch. As you sweep your arm, get all four sides:

   - From the shoulder coming out to the palm side of the hand
   - From the armpit down to the pinky finger side of the hand
   - From the shoulder coming down on the back of the hand
   - From the outer arm coming down to the thumb side of the hand

3. Repeat on the other arm.

4. Now work with your legs. If you are standing, set one foot on a chair and use both hands to sweep down all four sides of your leg and your foot.

5. Repeat on the other leg.

6. Sense your arms and legs. Do you find that they are filled up, three-dimensional and heavy, and making more contact with the ground?

7. Sweep the front of your body from shoulders, over your chest and belly, all the way down to your pelvis. Sweep the side of your chest and your back as best as you are able.

8. Very gently sweep your neck (front, back, and sides) and your face and head. Pull your ears up, down, out, and then forward and backward. This supports your vagus nerve, which we will discuss in more detail in the next chapter.

Notice if you are feeling more grounded, embodied, heavy, or settled. Is there any tingling or vibration? You may feel the need to yawn or notice tears in your eyes. These can all be signs of relaxation and groundedness.

🪷 Mindfulness Tool: Box Breathing to De-Stress

Did you know that Navy Seals use Box Breathing as a tool to stay calm in stressful situations? This rhythmic breathwork method combines relaxed breathing with concentration and mindfulness and may help you to avoid reactionary thinking or panic. If you can practice this daily in the morning for five to twenty minutes, your nervous system will be rewired to the slow, deep diaphragmatic breathing patterns that will keep you calm and relaxed in stressful situations.

It's important to note that not every mindfulness technique works for everyone. While Box Breathing was an effective tool for my client

Selma to work through her traumatic images, you may find that it has a different effect. Every person is different, and I will be offering more breathing techniques throughout this book so that you can find the one that suits you best.

1. Sit comfortably in a relaxed position with your back straight and upright. If you feel safe, then close your eyes and mouth and breathe only through your nose.
2. Exhale deeply to breathe out all the stale air in your lungs.
3. Breathe in through the nose, mentally counting to four (four seconds).
4. Now, hold your breath to the count of four and keep your chest lifted.
5. Breathe out to the count of four.
6. Hold your breath again to the count of four. This is one cycle.
7. Repeat this Box Breathing cycle slowly and effortlessly (inhale, hold, exhale, hold).

If you are gasping for breath when you hold your breath at the end of inhale and exhale, then eliminate the holding. You can start with a breath to the count of two and slowly work your way up to holding the breath to the count of four.

Notice if you feel calm after a few minutes of rhythmic breathing. For seasoned meditators, try incorporating the mantra "Om Mani Padme Hum" in place of each "one, two, three, four" count. Translated, the chant says that the jewel of compassion will unfold your lotus heart in the midst of the muddy waters of your daily life stressors. Another alternative is to say "Love, love, love, love" four times instead of counting.

Growing Stronger

According to the Noble Truths of Buddhism, we should understand that both suffering and our ability to heal from it are a part of life. That's not to say that the trauma in our life is necessarily fair or justified, it only means that when trauma does happen, we have the choice to decide what we want to do with it. In each of the client stories I shared, not a single one of them chose their trauma. They did, however, realize that their mind and their bodies were powerful tools in Noticing, Naming, Pausing, and Choosing Otherwise.

When we recognize that we have a choice in how we use our brains and our bodies, we are better equipped to move ourselves out of traumatic states and into a healthier and happier way of being. That may mean changing our thoughts and our beliefs about how our minds, bodies, and the world work. We are inherently wired to protect ourselves from danger. Noticing and seeking safety is important for our trauma healing.

Mindfulness is a powerful tool to help us build resilience in the face of trauma. Studies have shown that resilience[8] is associated with inner strength and competence,[9] optimism,[10] flexibility,[11] and the ability to cope effectively when faced with adversity.[12] Resilience also minimizes the impact of stressful life events. Resilient people develop qualities such as optimism, social support, and active coping, which in turn increase their ability to deal with life's challenges. By inviting us to live in the present moment, mindfulness can open us to infinite possibilities in the future. Remember that trauma is often a failure of imagination because when we are caught in trauma, we only expect the worst outcome for our future.

Mindfulness is a daily and lifelong practice. It is constantly weeding our gardens with care for what we are choosing to keep and what we do not wish to be a part of us. Mindfulness practices offer the challenge of feeling everything, but they also gift us with the benefit of being fully alive in our life. If we truly want to work through the traumas that we are holding, mindfulness may be an incredibly powerful path forward.

Your Body's Response to Danger and Safety

The energy of trauma can be transformed into the energy of life. . . .
It takes a lot of energy to keep the pain managed and suppressed.

—Gabor Maté

During my time as a successful professional in the business world, I paid attention to the types of candidates that my company hired and watched how they performed their jobs. I found it interesting that my company preferred military candidates who brought with them a "team first" mentality and seemed to consistently deliver strong performance. They knew how to survive and thrive in high-stress environments, thanks to years of training in controlling their nervous systems. They had developed resilient nervous systems.

Similarly, I heard of other financial management companies selecting candidates with experience in high-stress jobs because they were often better suited to make the right decision in difficult situations. That means someone who had experience as an air traffic controller might get preference over the straight-A graduate student for a job that requires quick decisions in high-stakes situations. Financial skills can be taught, but a calm and resilient nervous system is not part of on-the-job training.

We see evidence of strong nervous system regulation in elite athletes, like those who practice mixed martial arts, gymnastics, tennis, or boxing. We also see it in top chess players, who strategize multiple moves ahead while they're under tremendous pressure to win the match. For high-visibility athletes, like NFL players or Olympic athletes, there is increased pressure of performing at their peak level while they're under the watchful eye of millions of fans. Extreme sports enthusiasts, like mountain climbers, may not have an audience but face unique stresses due to weather or other natural conditions.

These athletes have trained their minds and bodies to thrive in conditions that most regular humans could not survive in. Through using mindfulness techniques, however, we can learn to balance our mind and body by controlling our stress response and building a resilient nervous system. Let's begin with a high-level overview of our nervous system.

Understanding Our Nervous System

Our bodies and minds are miraculously programmed with responses to help keep us safe or minimize the impact of the danger we're experiencing. Our nervous system is made up of the somatic nervous system and the autonomic nervous system. Our *somatic nervous system* is our conscious nervous system that controls voluntary movements like walking or blinking our eyes. The *autonomic nervous system* is in charge of all the automatic activities that we don't have to consciously think about doing like breathing, pumping blood, and digesting.

Within the autonomic nervous system, we can branch into two subcategories: the *sympathetic nervous system (SNS)* and the *parasympathetic nervous system (PNS)*. Our SNS is what energizes us in times of stress or danger. It is our fight, flight, or freeze response to situations; our pupils may dilate and digestion takes a back seat while we prepare to attack or run. Within our PNS we may experience rest and digest as our autonomic nervous system conserves energy and promotes relaxation.

Trauma resides within the autonomic nervous system. Once you understand that autonomic or automatic nervous system, you can use it to your advantage to work your way out of trauma. With trauma, the nervous system goes into high alert, and as a result, it affects our thoughts, emotions, body sensations, and behaviors. So let's understand how to consciously shift the outcome by identifying behaviors to control or hack our stress response.

Balancing the Sympathetic and Parasympathetic Nervous Systems

Maintaining a healthy balance between our stress response and our resting response is essential for reducing overall stress in our lives. In addition to deep breathing, physical care such as hydration, sleep, movement, and open-ended rest time are essential for a happy nervous system. The practices of love, kindness, compassion, gratitude, forgiveness, and joy for our own successes and the good fortune of others also support our nervous system.

Our SNS has an energizing effect, getting us out of bed in the morning, and helps us with activities like bathing, cooking, running to catch the bus, playing basketball, texting, scrolling on social media, and so on. Meanwhile, the PNS has a calming effect that helps us go to sleep, languish on the couch watching TV, read a book, relax during a massage, or enjoy a meal with loved ones.

What I find fascinating about our nervous system is that depending on how I approach any activity, I can turn on my SNS or PNS. For example, if I lazily walk over to the kitchen, pick up my cup of tea, and return to the sofa, slowly relishing every sip, I will drop into a PNS state. Instead, if I rush to the kitchen, grab my cup (likely spilling some tea in the process), and gulp it down, I've moved myself into SNS state. Almost any activity can be done in a relaxed state to change the state of my nervous system from stress to rest.

Why is this important? Consciously choosing how we approach things has the ability to affect the release of hormones in our bodies. When I am rushing around in an SNS state, then the stress hormones adrenaline (epinephrine) and cortisol are released, which activate my fight or flight response. Now, if I approached my entire day in this anxious state, I might find that I have a difficult time going to sleep because of my elevated level of cortisol. High cortisol can inhibit the work of another important hormone, melatonin, which is meant to help me sleep. The high cortisol and ineffective melatonin can increase my SNS at night, making me too restless to go to bed, so I may binge-watch TV or scroll through social media. The result is that I spend the night feeling both wired and exhausted. In my fatigued state, the cycle easily repeats itself day after day.

While it is helpful to have a basic understanding of our hormones and their purpose, we are unable to see, measure, or assess them to help us determine which nervous system is dominant in our body. What other indicators will help us recognize our dominant nervous system and empower us to change it? Instead of giving you an answer, I want you to try to guess which of the body functions are turned on during a fight, flight, or freeze response. Which functions are turned on if we are in a state of rest? Test yourself to see what signs you already know.

	Sympathetic NS (Fight, Flight, or Freeze)	Parasympathetic NS (Rest and Digest)
Heart Rate		
Respiration		
Vision		
Digestion		
Muscle Tone		
Immune System		
Cognition		

I want you to imagine you're running on a beautiful beach in Hawaii on a lovely, sunny day. Suddenly, a dog comes tearing down the beach, barking and chasing after you. Now, answer the following questions:

- **Heart Rate:** Is your heart beating fast?

- **Respiration:** Are you breathing fast and shallow in your upper chest and lungs?

- **Vision:** Are your eyes focused on your path and the dog, or are you looking around slowly, taking in the lapping ocean waves? Are your pupils dilated? You will take in more light and your surroundings with dilated pupils.

- **Digestion:** Would you consider eating your sandwich while running away from the dog? Is digestion still turned on in your body? One way to evaluate this is to check for saliva in your mouth. If your mouth is dry, then your digestion is most likely turned off.

- **Muscle Tone:** Are your muscles tensed and ready for running, with blood flow in your arms and legs?

- **Immune System:** While it is difficult to determine what your immune system is doing inside your body, what would you guess your body will do? Will it spend resources on cleaning and repairing and getting rid of harmful viruses and bacteria, or will it divert the resources to save you from being bitten?

- **Cognition:** Are you accessing just your short-term memory as you figure out how to outrun the dog? Or is this a moment for you to reminisce on your sacred oath to your beloved?

If your heart is beating hard, you are taking short and quick breaths, your eyes are focused and dilated, your muscles are ready, your mouth is dry and immune systems are shut down, and you are accessing only short-term memory, then you are in SNS response. Yes, you are stressed and running for your life, and the SNS is turned on to help you either fight the dog or run away from it. These hurried and stressed states are common in our busy lives.

Accessing short-term memory when we are stressed is fine for emergencies, and it even works for doom-scrolling on social media as you watch a short video, then watch another and forget what the first one was about. The difficulty is if this becomes a constant way of life. It creates wear and tear on the body, which can have long-term adverse health effects. Remember, during a stressed SNS state, your immune and digestive systems are not working at their fullest.

Let's reinvent the previous scenario (in case your body is still feeling like that dog is after you). Imagine yourself back on that vacation in Hawaii. This time, you're watching the vibrant sunset from your balcony. You can hear waves lapping in the distance, and every so often, you notice the sweet scent of plumeria wafting through the air. Your eyes are rested and unfocused or maybe looking at the waves crashing gently on the beach. Your heart rate is slowed, and you are breathing deeply. The muscles of your arms and legs are relaxed and heavy. You most likely have saliva in your mouth, indicating that your digestion is active. As you sit and watch the sunset, memories of the recent or distant past might come to mind. You are in your PNS. This is a great state to be in for learning and retaining knowledge in your long-term memory bank.

If you still feel unclear about how the SNS and PNS work when they're active, I've included a completed table here.

	Sympathetic NS (Fight, Flight, or Freeze)	Parasympathetic NS (Rest and Digest)
Heart Rate	Increase	Decrease
Respiration	Increase	Decrease
Vision	Dilated	Soft eyes
Digestion	Shuts down	Online
Muscle Tone	Blood is diverted from the skin periphery (pale, cold) to prepare for potential injury. Blood is diverted to muscles for quicker movement.	Blood flow returns to the skin and is diverted away from muscles, so muscle tension releases and the body relaxes.
Immune System	Shuts down	Fully turned on
Cognition	Short term	Long term

Before we delve some more into our nervous system, let's take a break to turn on our PNS so that we can absorb new information and store it in our long-term memory. Come back to mindfulness exercises, like this one, whenever you are preparing to engage in a task where having your long-term memory would be useful, like studying for a test or sitting in an important board meeting.

☸ Mindfulness Tool: Using Your Relief Resources

In this practice, we begin to recognize how our body feels when we are relaxed vs when going into fight, flight, or freeze. Our sense of safety plays a significant role in our body's relaxation response.

Take a few moments to recall or revisit the Your Relief Resources Inventory Mindfulness Tool in chapter one. These are activities you engage in when you are relaxed, such as singing, dancing, working out, or watching movies.

Now, remember a time when you were deeply relaxed and engaged in one of these activities. Write down your PNS symptoms based on the table. Notice the saliva in your mouth and the softness in your eyes. As your relaxation starts to fade, remember another time when you were happy and relaxed. For example, if, when you are working out in the gym, you are relaxed and have SNS symptoms of muscles being fully engaged, write that down. We have this idea that relaxing just means engaging in inert activities (high PNS) like watching TV or sex or sleeping but let's expand our body's understanding of relaxation that can come from engaging in active activities (high SNS) like exercise or running. The common thread here is that you were feeling safe and your body is relaxed during this activity. While feeling safe, you can either have your SNS or PNS be engaged. The SNS or PNS are engaged during your stress response, but are turned on when we are relaxed and safe too. If your breathing is deep and relaxed and body feels heavy and grounded and there's saliva in your mouth, that's a sign that your body feels is feeling safe.

Hacking Your Nervous System

Let's delve deeper into understanding and hacking your nervous system. If I asked you to sit on the floor, close your eyes, and meditate quietly for an hour, what would your response be? For some of you, it might sound awful to have to sit without movement or any form of engagement. Your skin might feel prickly, and feelings of anxiety might heighten at the thought of participating in something where you may feel like a prisoner in your own body. Or perhaps you have the opposite response to being asked to sit still. You may feel so tired or low energy that the thought of sitting for an hour and not having to "do" anything feels like a welcomed reprieve. Perhaps you'd even ask permission to fully recline for the meditation. Holding your body in a seated upright position might still feel like too much exertion.

Why is it that for some of us, being asked to sit still feels like the equivalent of being asked to sit on top of an active volcano, while others of us feel that the act of sitting for a prolonged period feels so good? This has to do with the predominant nervous system we operate in during our daily life. Are you someone who has a lot of anxious energy, or do you prefer moving around while you're thinking? Do you work well under deadlines and think fast, sometimes so fast that you have a hard time sitting down to accomplish your tasks because you're multitasking and you have a lot of nervous energy? We call this high *sympathetic tone* or hyperarousal. If, instead, you struggle with motivation to leap into action and find that you are inclined to binge Netflix on the couch all day, or if you love constant snacking and resting, then it's likely you have a high *parasympathetic tone* and experience hypoarousal. Take a moment to identify which feels more like your own nervous system response to your daily life stressors.

Our autonomic nervous system responds to stressors in different ways, which means that we need different tools to help manage and regulate ourselves. If you are a person with hyperarousal, having things like movement and deadlines is absolutely essential to your process. Movement, like walking or stretching, might help to abate your nervous energy. If you are able to sit in front of your computer and focus your eyes with mindfulness for a few minutes, this uncomfortable hyper energy may peak and burst within you like fireworks. Then your mind will calm down, and you will be able to focus.

If you have hypoarousal, then you might find that your breath is already slow and deep. It may be too slow and too deep, taking you into a deep parasympathetic state and contributing to your sluggish feelings. One of the fastest ways to come out of this state is through a technique called Bellows Breath. In this breathwork practice, you sit with your back straight, inhale fast through the nose, and exhale equally quickly through the nose. This is a practice the ancients discovered thousands of years ago to move them out of sluggish states of mind and body, which the Buddhists call sloth and torpor.

Bellows Breath is similar to the Wim Hof Method,[13] where you breathe in sharply through the nose and let the breath out unforced in rapid succession. Doing one to five minutes of Bellows Breath or a similar method might energize you to the point where you feel like you can take on more activity. Singing or chanting can be energizing too. As you generate more energy, you can begin to work with movement, like exercise or dancing, to keep your energy higher and more balanced.

Approaching your nervous system with a sense of curiosity is like holding the key to your own mental, emotional, and physical health. When you can recognize the behaviors and patterns of your nervous system, then it becomes fun to explore ways to engage with it to best support yourself. It also allows you greater perception into the nervous system state of your partner, your children, your friends, or your co-workers. When you understand them better, you are less inclined to fight with them and more inclined to meet them where they are. This is how you affect positive change in your life.

🪷 Mindfulness Tool: Restoring Safety in the Body

Since the basis of stress is a feeling of lack of safety, let's practice restoring a sense of safety in our body and develop resilience. This exercise primarily uses our sense of sight. According to science, your eyes are simply brain tissue on the outside. Once the eyes focus, the brain starts to calm down and settle. When we bring focus to our eyes, the mind comes into focus too. This is a trick meditators have known for a few thousand years. They use a *drishti*—an intentional focal point—to mindfully focus their eyes internally or externally. This can be done during stillness, during slow movement like yoga, or even during fast movement, like the whirling dervishes who meditate by dancing in circles to ascend into a deep state of bliss.

As you are going through this exercise, pay attention to the level of saliva in your mouth. More saliva is an indication that your nervous system may be moving into parasympathetic rest and digest. You may also notice yourself taking a deep sigh, swallowing, or yawning.

1. Start out by sitting in a comfortable chair and evaluate your current state of relaxation by using a Resilience Scale from 0 to 10, with 0 being highly stressed and 10 becoming completely relaxed.

2. Slowly look around the room you are in. Notice and name the objects you see.

3. Begin to touch different textures in the space around you. Notice the feel of your soft, fuzzy pillow, the cold smoothness of your kitchen countertop, or the rough ridges of your jeans. If it feels safe, close your eyes as you touch various textures so that you are only experiencing sensations.

4. With each thing you observe via sight or touch, challenge yourself to engage with the space with curiosity or a beginner's mind. Just as a baby learns by putting everything in its mouth, explore your familiar space as if you're experiencing it for the first time.

5. Notice any changes in your breath. Taking deep breaths is one indication that you are restoring your parasympathetic nervous system to a place of safety within your being.

6. When you are done with the exercise, revisit your Resilience Scale and notice if you feel more relaxed.

Our Emotional Response to Fight, Flight, or Freeze

Now that we have restored a sense of safety in our body, let's delve a little deeper into our stress response of fight, flight, or freeze. When we are unable to move out of or extinguish our stress response, then our body may get stuck in these responses. We experience emotional symptoms as a result of our stress responses. For example, when our SNS remains mobilized for fight or flight, the following emotional symptoms may appear:

- Chronic stress
- Impulsive behavior
- Difficulty thinking clearly
- Feeling out of control, worried, or fearful
- Feeling angry, enraged, or overwhelmed, sometimes without knowing why
- Getting irritated or confrontational with others
- Feeling panicked or ready to run

I have learned to catch myself early on. As the SNS is starting to mobilize, I use the Restoring Safety in the Body Mindfulness Tool to calm the sympathetic tone. When I am feeling worried or frustrated, I practice NNPCO so that I don't end up at the other end of the spectrum with feelings of panic or rage. This helps reduce potential harm to my relationships with those around me as I choose a different way of expressing myself. Additional strategies to de-escalate the SNS and bring calmness to our mind and heart are listed later in this chapter.

Freeze is the next level of stress response and can occur when we feel that we are unable to escape a stressful situation with fight or flight, so we resort to collapse or shutdown. This is a go-to response for babies; when they're unable to communicate discomfort, babies will suddenly go quiet after a deep, despairing cry.

As adults, when we start to enter a freeze response, we may notice that our heart rate and body temperature decrease. We're also less likely to make eye contact in social situations and we are not attuned to vocal prosody or nuances of the human voice. So, if a friend is trying to comfort me when I am dissociated or in a freeze, I may not pick up cues about their care and my safety.

When our nervous system moves into a freeze state, the following emotional symptoms may appear:

- Unhealthy coping mechanisms
- Feeling trapped, disconnected, dark, numb, hopeless, helpless, shutdown, shame, despair, depressed

When we are in freeze, we may feel physically exhausted and emotionally numb, and the simple pleasures of life, like food, may not feel satisfying. We may feel disconnected from our loved ones. Freeze can be a state of extreme despair and can be a very distressing state to experience. You need the warmth of human contact to move out of it, but you are also unable to receive the connection you need. This response is slow to shift, and being patient with yourself is helpful in moving it out.

If you feel a state of freeze coming on, I suggest making extra effort to be in the presence of loved ones and receive hugs. I also strongly encourage working with a professional therapist who can help bring you out of this state, particularly if your situation is related to childhood trauma. In addition, I suggest using some strategies, such as the Restoring Safety in the Body Mindfulness Tool for moving the parasympathetic tone. Remember to be slow and gentle with yourself while moving the freeze response. It's best not to rush yourself when this response is present.

Having someone support you and love you back into human connection is essential. Sometimes, this state is diagnosed as depression, and medications are prescribed. While I support medication, it does not address the underlying emotions in the freeze state. There may be grief or childhood trauma underlying this shutdown state, which needs to be addressed and met with love. Love is a powerful healer to nurse someone out of freeze state so that they can enjoy the simple joys of life. Here is a story from my life:

My father passed away when I was a teenager, sending me into a state of shock. While I always felt a sense of urgency to get home and support my ailing mother, my dear friend Pervin would lovingly and persistently invite me over to her home so that she could nurture me with delicious food. When I relaxed with a satiated belly, she would draw me out of my painful emotional state. After these serious conversations, we would enjoy music, laugh, and tease each other.

Her friendship protected me from a full-blown freeze shutdown and gave me the capacity to still be there for my grieving mother. When Pervin left for Hong Kong two years later, I turned over my care to a therapist and traveled several hours to see him three times a week. Pervin went on to become a powerful healer and has run Shakti

Healing Center in downtown Hong Kong for almost two decades. I still tease her that I was her first practice client and her first success.

In the olden times, family members were our therapists, and we listened to each other's pain and suffering. Our ancestors gathered around the fire at night and told stories to each other, which helped metabolize their stress and trauma. The Navajo people used to gather around a person who was ailing and thank them for reflecting to the community that they were not being sufficiently supported.[14] The community would leave their work in the fields to support the ailing person with ceremony and ritual until their soul returned to them. We might interpret this as meaning that the person came out of their freeze state and returned to feeling the joy and aliveness of life. Speaking with a beloved friend, support group, trusted therapist, mentor, or teacher is essential to help us come out of freeze state.

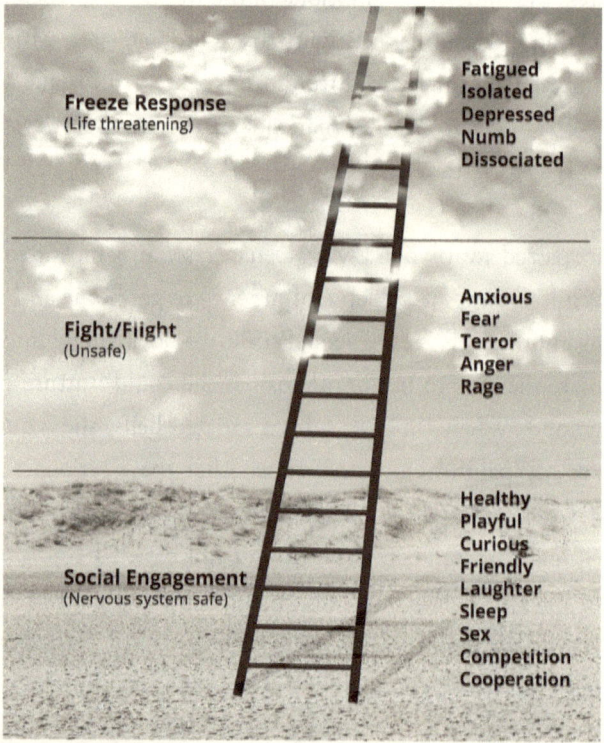

Freeze Response
(Life threatening)

Fatigued
Isolated
Depressed
Numb
Dissociated

Fight/Flight
(Unsafe)

Anxious
Fear
Terror
Anger
Rage

Social Engagement
(Nervous system safe)

Healthy
Playful
Curious
Friendly
Laughter
Sleep
Sex
Competition
Cooperation

☼ Mindfulness Tool: Moving Out of Freeze State

If the traumatic state persists or is exacerbated, the ladder of arousal moves us from a state of calm into fight or flight, and then into freeze (see image above). If we are in a freeze state and coming back down the ladder of arousal, we may run into fight or flight response emotions such as anger, rage, fear, or terror. While these emotions may not feel good, they are actually a good sign. They mean that we are moving in the right direction. Coming out of freeze is a nonlinear process, which means that you may come out of freeze temporarily but then slide back into it. It can be quite disorienting to work through, so having a therapist to support you in this journey will be helpful.

Here are some suggested movements to be done slowly with several rest breaks.

- Slowly move fingers and toes
- Slowly look around the room you are in and orient yourself to the space
- Rest often but stay connected with your body and breath
- Gently move your body in ways that feel good to you, like walking, dancing, or even blinking or swallowing
- Orient yourself toward safety, even if it's momentary safety, by remembering a time you felt safe in your home or in someone's presence
- Receive hugs from loved ones
- Sweep your own body with love and gratitude to help you feel more embodied as you did in the Mindfulness Tool of sweeping your body in chapter two.

Notice if your body feels more relaxed and safe. If you had to subjectively rate your relaxation on a Resilience Scale from 0 to 10, with 0 being stressed and 10 being entirely relaxed, how would you rate your current state of well-being? It may be difficult to do a self-assessment if you're in an active state of freeze, so be patient with yourself and keep a journal to document your progress each time you go through this exercise.

Using Meditation to Work with a Fight, Flight, or Freeze Response

There are three potential pitfalls to be aware of when using meditation while you're working with trauma in your nervous system. The first of these is spiritual bypass. *Spiritual bypass* can show up as avoiding or ignoring the fight and flight responses because it does not feel acceptable to our definition of a good meditation student. You may ignore the frustration, irritation, anger, or rage that are a natural part of a fight response. But bypassing these feelings can send you higher up the ladder of arousal into a state of freeze.

You may find yourself quick to forgive or ignore things that are important to you to avoid acknowledging your real feelings. Meditators have a difficult time with intense emotion as they don't fit well with the calm and harmony we seek. But if you take these difficult emotions as your growing edge, then you can learn to have difficult conversations and set boundaries without escalating the situation. I want to share the insight Basil had when he discovered the power of using mindfulness meditation to release his relentless trauma symptoms:

Basil was dealing with constant anxiety for a few weeks and had many sleepless nights, which exacerbated his quality of life during the day. He felt a constant tightness in his solar plexus, brought on by old relationship patterns that made him feel claustrophobic and trapped.

As a regular meditator, Basil tried to manage his anxiety with his usual meditation practice by awareness of sensation, thoughts, and emotions. Unlike other experiences he had worked through with meditation, he realized that what he was doing was not a means to get rid of anxiety. Why? Because meditation is about being present with what you're feeling, not erasing it. Basil had to be willing to sit with his anxiety and body tightness and offer it as much self-compassion as he could muster. Just this realization of how meditation works helped melt his tight solar plexus so that his breath could flow and his body and mind could relax.

I share just a brief snippet of Basil's story to illustrate an important part of choosing mindfulness meditation to work with trauma: meditation is about being present. Choosing meditation as a healing tool means sitting with our pain, distressing emotions, and recursive thoughts with self-love and self-compassion. When we surround ourselves with our own warmth, it's possible for our symptoms to sometimes release.

Additionally, if you are choosing meditation as a tool to help you out of fight, flight, or freeze, I would encourage you to also make sure that you have outside support from professionals, friends, or family. Remember, trauma is healed in the warm, caring, and loving presence of another person. We cannot DIY our healing entirely.

Another potential challenge to be aware of when using meditation is that trauma symptoms are sometimes enhanced when eyes are closed. If your SNS is overactive and you force your body to sit still in meditation with your eyes closed, it is possible that your symptoms may get exacerbated. Instead, I encourage you to seek ways to meditate with your eyes open, even if that means looking down to minimize sensory input. Choose a meditation practice that is in harmony with your nervous system, not working against it.

This brings us to our third challenge: choosing to use stationary meditation techniques without movement. When we are in an acute state of fight, flight, or freeze, it is beneficial for us to move our bodies. If you are meditating by sitting or lying in stillness on the floor, you may be at odds with your nervous system if you're also experiencing activating imagery or memories at that time. Those visions can create a high level of energy in the body that is best managed through movement. I suggest honoring your body with movement such as a walk, hike, or run. When the energetic response to memories or thoughts is extinguished in the body with the help of movement, then you may return to a practice in stillness.

☯ Mindfulness Tool: Restoring Safety with Sound

Since the fight, flight, and freeze responses are triggered due to the inner feeling of lack of safety, here is another practice to help restore a sense of safety in your body. Sound is one way that we can mindfully orient ourselves to our space and our present senses.

1. Start by sitting comfortably on a chair in your room where you already feel safe. Close your eyes and breath for a few minutes. You don't need to change your breathing, just breathe in whatever way feels natural to you.

2. Check in with your Resilience Scale and notice where your relaxation level is from 0 to 10, with 0 being highly stressed and 10 being completely relaxed.

3. Feel your feet on the floor. Curl your toes and release them a few times as if you are trying to pick up a pencil from the floor. Notice how this affects your breath. Next, lift your toes a few times and set them down. Do you feel more grounded and more in contact with the floor?

4. Keeping your eyes closed, listen to the sounds inside the room. You may hear your own breathing, sounds inside your body, the thrumming of the refrigerator, or the whirring of a fan.

5. Shift your attention to sounds outside the room. This may be the sweet sounds of birds chirping or the hum of an airplane. Bring

the curiosity of your beginner's mind to the exercise, as if you are hearing these sounds for the first time in your life.

6. Return your focus back to sounds inside your space and then again shift to listening outside of your immediate space. We are activating your inner ear muscles in this exercise.

7. Bring this exercise to a close by noticing if your feet and legs feel more grounded. Check in with the depth of your breath.

8. Check with your Resilience Scale and see whether you've moved the needle of your relaxation a little higher. If yes, then you have moved into your PNS, your rest and digest response. Wonderful job!

When Our Bodies Perceive Danger at All Times

Students often ask me why their nervous systems stay in a state of fight, flight, or freeze long after an initial trauma has happened. In my teachings, I share that our heart's deepest desire is to have connection with the people around us and to live in a conflict-free world. Many of my students have that well-known "Coexist" bumper sticker on their cars, and yet they still face the daily stress and feelings of anger or fear from people and events around them. If they are actively working toward peace, why do they retain heightened alert states in their minds and bodies?

To understand this we need to look at Paul MacLean's theory on the triune brain.[15] MacLean believed that our brain operated like three brains: the brain stem or the reptilian complex (automatic functions of breathing; heart rate; and survival responses of fight, flight, or freeze), the limbic system (emotions), and the neocortex (speech, logic, planning, strategizing, and higher thinking). While MacLean's theory has been criticized for oversimplifying the brain systems, it is helpful for our purpose of understanding our stress response.

I briefly introduced the amygdala (part of our limbic system) to you in chapter two while discussing the Second Noble Truth. When we perceive something as unsafe, our amygdala leaps into action. It quickly scans through our database of past experiences and determines whether we are in danger or not. If it determines a threat, our brain stem gets activated and we launch into fight, flight, or freeze. These decisions and activations are made within nanoseconds and without our conscious thought.

The challenge today is that our amygdala can't always differentiate which threats are genuinely life-threatening and which are just stimuli that we can let go. In some ways, our nervous systems are still responding like they did with our ancient ancestors, where the sound of a stick breaking might necessitate immediate response to avoid being attacked by a saber-toothed tiger. Our body hasn't evolved much from our cave-dwelling ancestors, but our environment has changed tremendously in terms of what we perceive as a threat. The amygdala cannot necessarily determine if a stressful board meeting, dangerous driver, or being late to get your child from school are manageable stressors or life-threatening. So, it turns on the full-blown fight, flight, or freeze response as if you were being chased by a saber-toothed tiger or a wooly mammoth. Given the nearly constant barrage of stressful inputs in our life, with far less time for rest, our overactive amygdala sends us into a constant state of heightened alertness.

As we learn how to calm down our amygdala and regulate our nervous system, we not only move through traumatic experiences, but are calm and grounded in everyday life. Remember that when our amygdala feels threatened, it does not consult with our thinking brain or the neocortex for the best and most logical decisions. When we are stressed, we are not at our most charming or creative self.

Learning to calm your stress response increases your access to a higher level of thinking and processing, allowing you to see more options and make better choices. The following exercise helps connect the reptilian brain with the thinking brain so that we can use our logic to calm our stress response. It will help balance your brain, which will in turn help balance your body.

🪷 Mindfulness Tool: Calming Our Trauma Response

Here is a practice to calm our reptilian brain (brain stem) and turn on our thinking brain (prefrontal cortex).[16]

1. Sit comfortably on a chair or a sofa. Check your Resilience Scale and see how relaxed or stressed you're feeling at the moment.

2. Place one hand on your forehead (prefrontal cortex) and the other hand at the back of your head with the palm covering the dent where your head connects to your neck. This is the occiput area, where your brain stem is located. When your arms get tired, I suggest you switch your hands. Holding for a few minutes is usually sufficient and the tiredness of your arms is a good signal to release the hold. If you can't hold your arms above your head for a few minutes, then ask someone to do this hold for you.

3. Check in with your breath and notice if there is any improvement in your Resilience Scale. If there is any improvement in the Resilience Scale, that's a good signal your trauma response has calmed down and your thinking brain is back online.

The Window of Tolerance

I want you to think back to the beginning of this book and your goal in reading it. Chances are that you chose a goal of coherence or integrating your body, brain, and heart to handle life's challenges with greater resilience. According to Dr. Dan Siegel, founder and executive director of education at the Mindsight Institute, *coherence* means linking the three parts of us (body, brain, and heart) through synaptic connections. Siegel says, "These integrated linkages enable more intricate functions to emerge—such as insight, empathy, intuition, and morality. A result of integration is kindness, resilience, and health. Terms for these three forms of integration are a coherent mind, empathic relationships, and an integrated brain."[17]

When we are in coherence, both our sympathetic and parasympathetic nervous systems are working in harmony, and they are operating within the *window of tolerance*, which means there is optimal arousal in our nervous system.

In a healthy nervous system, the SNS and PNS cycle within the bounds of the functional range where they balance each other out. Both nervous systems are turned on throughout the day. While you sleep, you are in a deep PNS cycle and when you wake up, the SNS energizes you and gets you out of your bed. When you are living within the boundaries of this window of tolerance and have a sense of safety, you are living in the *social engagement* nervous system, a term coined by the psychologist Stephen Porges.[18] This is the regular life you desire to live when you feel safe, relaxed, and energized, and you are *not* in a stress response.

The interesting thing is that you can still enter moments of fight, flight, or freeze when you feel safe, just as you do when you feel unsafe. The underlying key is safety! When you feel unsafe and go into fight, flight, or freeze, you are entering the world of stress and trauma. When you feel safe and engage in these responses, you are in the social engage-

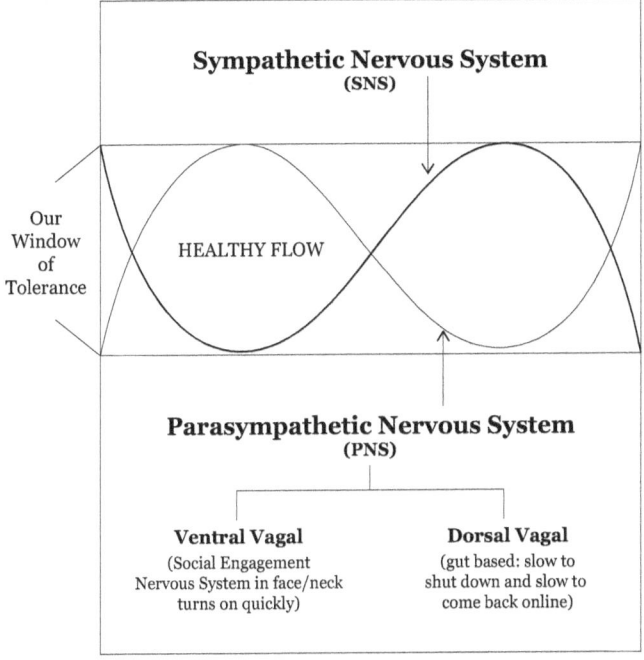

Nervous System – High Level Overview
- Sympathetic Nervous System
- Parasympathetic Nervous System
  - Ventral Vagal
  - Dorsal Vagal

ment nervous system. For example, when you're in your safe zone, you may experience the immobility of a freeze response during sleep or sex. When you're playing sports, you are engaging in safe and friendly fight or flight response. Your SNS response is what allows you to play harder or run faster during these activities, but your mind and heart will be filled with joy and the excitement of competition if you're coming from a place of social engagement rather than the stress of trauma. The sense of safety of engaging in these activities keeps you within the window of tolerance. When you witness firsthand the effect of your thoughts, emotions, and bodily sensations in creating your sense of safety, then you may be motivated to be more mindful and selective about them.

Whether we're with friends having a good time or in a stressful meeting, our nervous system is always responding to cues of safety and cues of danger in our environment (*neuroception*). Based on these cues, we either live in the playful and joyful social engagement within the window of tolerance, or we are launched into a stress response of fight, flight, or freeze.

The challenge with our body is that our amygdala does not differentiate between recollection of past trauma versus a present event—it experiences both of them as equally threatening and responds by turning on a full-blown fight, flight, or freeze response. This is known as faulty neuroception. That is why you can be in the safety of your home engaged in a safe activity, like feeding your baby, but if you're thinking about your angry boss or remembering the fender bender you had earlier that day, your nervous system will trigger your stress response. This will send you up the ladder of arousal from your safe social engagement to fight or flight and potentially into a dissociation or freeze response. This may also happen when you're watching the news or a show with violence, which is why if you are already feeling particularly stressed and your nervous system is outside of the window of tolerance, then I suggest that you be especially careful about what type of media you consume.

There are two ways to protect ourselves from faulty neuroception. One way is to make it conscious by using mindful orientation, covered in the first chapter, to bring our awareness to our surrounding sights, sounds, and smells. This practice reinforces a sense of safety and tames the faulty neuroception. The second way is to activate the vagus nerve, which turns on our social engagement nervous system and brings us within the window of tolerance. The *vagus nerve* is the longest cranial nerve in our body and innervates nearly all of our organs. The following is a Mindfulness Tool on ways to activate the vagus nerve.

☸ Mindfulness Tool: Calming the Vagus Nerve

Here are several simple exercises to activate and calm your vagus nerve.

- **Tapping** is very easy and can be done at any time, but it is best to do it in the morning and evening as maintenance but before your trauma symptoms arise. Gently tap your face, head, and neck. When you feel more comfortable, you can tap all over your body. The key is to have fun and not make this an exercise! A full tapping script is included in chapter 7.

- **Deep breathing** into the belly can help reduce the stress hormone cortisol. When we use deep breathing with a longer exhale, it activates our social engagement nervous system. Use a technique called 4-6-8-6 breath, where you inhale to a count of four, hold to a count of six, exhale to a count of eight, and then hold to a count of six. I suggest you try a shorter count, such as 2-3-4-3, so that you don't feel out of breath and slowly build up to the 4-6-8-6 breath.

- **Ear pulls** create more space for the vagus nerve endings near your ears. Stand in front of a mirror and gently hold your ears with your fingers. Slowly pull your ears in all directions.

- **Om or Aum chanting** out loud can activate the vagus nerve relaxation response. Start with one to two rounds in the morning and build up to ten to fifteen rounds of Om chanting for deep relaxation.

- **Laughter** not only helps activate the vagus nerve, but it can help you feel connected to others.

- **Humming or singing** move the vagus nerve in the throat and promote overall relaxation.

Balancing Feelings of Danger and Safety

Remember that trauma does not live in the event itself. Trauma lives in our nervous system, which is why people may respond differently to the same traumatic event. We cannot change the events that have happened to us, but we can work to care for our nervous system and free ourselves from the traumatic pain. We can de-escalate the state of our nervous system and learn to build a resilient one. It is incredibly empowering when we witness our own ability to affect our thoughts, emotions, and bodily sensations. Our own nervous system energy, in turn, has an influence on those around us by calming others when we feel calm and irritating others when we feel irritated.

The resiliency of our nervous system lies in its ability to return to feeling safe and connected after a traumatic event. Our resiliency determines the extent of our trauma response and how long it might take to come out of it.[19]

Dr. Peter Levine created Somatic Experiencing, a technique that helps build a resilient nervous system by alternately working in both our trauma vortex and our healing vortex. Our *trauma vortex* is where we feel the various physical and emotional symptoms that trap us in cycles of dysregulation due to our trauma. Our healing vortex is the counter rhythm to the trauma vortex. In this healing vortex, we process and heal from trauma by focusing on bodily sensations and restoring the natural ability of our nervous system to self-regulate and return to the safety and wholeness of social engagement.

When Peter works with others, or even when he has shared stories of his own traumatic past while teaching with me, he balances one cycle of trauma with one cycle of healing. That might look like first sharing his story of comfort, connection, and safety as a child waking up to his parents' surprise gift of a much-awaited toy train. After he experiences the excitement and joy of this memory, he then shares his traumatic event. He ends with balancing his nervous system by returning to the precious memory of himself as a young boy lost in playing with his toy train. After his traumatic sharing, this is an act of self-soothing and bringing himself back into balance. The Using Your Relief Resources Mindfulness Tool previously discussed in this chapter is equivalent to Peter's healing vortex.

This movement between the trauma and healing vortex is similar to the energetic flow between our sympathetic and parasympathetic nervous systems within the bounds of the window of tolerance. This is the safe haven of social engagement. Similar to Peter Levine, we can work at maintaining a balance and movement between our trauma and healing energies. We can enjoy physical care activities like staying hydrated, getting enough sleep, moving our bodies, and partaking in open-ended resting time. We can feed our mental and spiritual health through deeply resourceful states of love, kindness, joy, and compassion. We can work through our challenging emotions with gratitude, patience, self-compassion, and forgiveness.

Our consciousness and very existence desire balance, but as we go through life, events can throw us off. The wonderful news is that we can often bring ourselves back into harmony by cultivating a balance between being active and resting. This will trauma-proof us against future life events and build our resilience, our ability to have a soft body and soft heart in the midst of the vagaries of life.

PART TWO

Discovering Your Buddhist Personality Type

A New Lens for Healing

Being human is not about being any one particular way; it is about being as life creates you—with your own particular strengths and weaknesses, gifts and challenges, quirks and oddities.

—Kristin Neff

Reigniting your power and working through your trauma has a lot to do with your internal environment. Part one offered new ways to become consciously aware of your nervous system and lovingly accept your feelings and behaviors, including many tools to help guide you back into the window of tolerance when you're feeling out of balance. In this chapter, I want to offer you a perspective on the way you view and move through your world. I find this information to be immensely helpful in making sense of how and why I approach situations—including my own experiences of trauma—in the way that I do. It also opens my heart to understanding and accepting the many ways that other people in my life experience the world. The result is an increased capacity for love and compassion.

I would like for us to explore what it feels like to identify our experiences as being one of three flavors: pleasant, unpleasant, and neutral. The pleasant flavor experiences are the ones you want to move toward. These are activities you like, ones that give you joy and feed your soul— you want more of them. Conversely, the unpleasant flavor experiences are the things you avoid or feel an aversion toward, including your stressors and trauma symptoms. Lastly, neutral flavor experiences are all of the things in your world that don't particularly grab your attention. It may be the color of the walls in a room or billboards along the highway. You have an awareness of these things, but they aren't loud enough to distract you from working at your desk or driving on the road. A neutral flavor could also be the style of clothing you wear to avoid standing out at work or in a crowd.

☾ Mindfulness Tool: Working with Difficult Experiences Using the Three Flavors

Let's use your nascent knowledge of the three flavors of experiences in this series of exercises that should be done together fully, in sequence. As with Peter Levine's trauma and healing vortex work, these three exercises are designed to address the stress and trauma in a heightened state of the nervous system and then return it to a calm state. Give yourself thirty to forty-five minutes for this exercise, and please do not take any shortcuts here!

Part 1

1. **Check in:** Begin by checking in with your Resilience Scale from 0 to 10, with 0 being not at all relaxed and 10 being extremely relaxed.

2. **Consciously connect:** Sit comfortably in a room where you will have privacy for the entire thirty to forty-five minutes when practicing this mindfulness tool. Bring in an awareness of your true nature of *sat-chit-ananda*, that blue sky that always exists regardless of the weather. Connecting to *sat-chit-ananda* may look different for each person, but it is always about knowing that no matter what the circumstances are in your life, at the quantum level, you are loving awareness. Your true nature is truth, consciousness, and bliss.

3. **Observe:** Mindfully orient yourself to your space. Look around the room slowly. Then close your eyes and name three objects in the space, noting their shape and color. Open your eyes and look around the room once again. Notice if you are feeling more present and safe in the environment.

4. **Shake:** Begin incorporating movement by shaking your arms and legs for a couple of minutes, as if you were shaking off water. When you stop shaking, become aware of how your limbs feel with the movement.

5. **Envision:** Imagine how your authentic self, the one that feels safe, trusting, calm, and carefree, would like to move.

6. **Feel your body:** Sense your body and see how it feels. Notice your breath.

7. **Unpleasant flavor:** Bring up an unpleasant emotion, such as frustration, anger, or sadness. Start with a low-intensity emotion so that you can practice before moving to more intense or deep emotions. Notice where you sense the emotion in your body and what it feels like.

8. **Express:** If you did not have any inhibitions about someone watching you, how would you express this emotion? Does a movement arise in your body to express the emotion or is there a sound? Imagine making the movement or hearing the sound of you expressing this unpleasant emotion.

9. **Check in:** Check within to see whether the unpleasant emotion has released from your body. Naming sensations is difficult, as we don't often use sensation language. A way to make this more tangible is to look for simple sensations that represent each element: fire: warm/cool, earth: heavy/light, water: flow/stuck/tight, air: tingling/vibration. This process of sensing and interpreting signals in the body allows our nervous system to rewire and make sense of our experience.

Sensing our inner world is called *interoception*. When we practice interoception in a safe and controlled environment, we can relearn healthier responses to our emotional patterns. Be patient and give yourself a few minutes before moving to the next step.

1. **Pleasant flavor:** Now, either imagine (or do) some movement or make a sound that feels pleasant and that expresses your authentic self.

2. **Let go:** Ask yourself how your mind, body, and spirit can further let go of the difficult emotion you are working with. Is it through shaking your body and hands and feet, by bouncing or dancing, or making some sounds to express the emotion?

3. **Neutral flavor:** Look around you and find neutral colors or objects. Spend time looking at the neutral space and notice your body's reaction to the neutral flavor. Allow yourself some time for your mind to relax.

Part 2

Practice the One Minute Mindfulness exercise from chapter two.

Part 3

Practice the NNPCO exercise from chapter two using the specific experience from this exercise. Finally, check in with your Resilience Scale one more time and notice if your number has shifted.

The Buddhist Personality Types

Let's now understand your unique Buddhist personality type. There are many ways in which we can learn more about our personality traits and the lens through which we experience the world. I've heard my students tie their behaviors or preferences to their astrological signs, Enneagram typology, or Myers-Briggs personality types. There are many systems and beliefs that serve the purpose of helping make sense of who we are and why we do what we do. Though they were first presented in a foundational fifth-century Buddhist text (the *Visuddhimagga*, or *The Path of Purification*), the Buddhist personality types[20] are an incredibly insightful lens when it comes to understanding *why* we experience flavors of experiences in the way we do. The three types are:

- Greed

- Aversive

- Deluded

When I was first introduced to this typology, I was a bit put off by the harsh labels and wasn't sure that I wanted to explore more. I also noticed that as I read through each type, I could find reflections of myself in each one. How was I supposed to know my type if they all seemed to fit me in certain ways?

This, I soon learned, is the beauty of the Buddhist personality types—all three live in all of us. I now picture it like three colored lenses: red, yellow, and blue. All colors in the world are variations of how these three colored lenses interplay with each other. How they are layered creates the nuances between a purple that is lilac, a purple that leans toward magenta, and a purple that is closer to indigo. Can you see how this mirrors the people of this Earth? We are all somewhere on this spectrum depending on how our three Buddhist personality types are layered.

As far as my distaste for the names of the Buddhist personality types, I got curious with my feelings toward them and my desire not to be labeled as any of them. Using the NNPCO framework, I realized that they were just words and that I had the freedom to redefine them in a more neutral or even pleasant way. For the sake of this chapter, I will provide both the traditional labels used and my own preferred descriptors for each of the personality types. (And once you understand my personality type, you may have a greater understanding of why I chose this approach!)

Buddhist Personality as It Relates to Trauma Healing

Our Buddhist personality is a way to develop a better understanding of ourselves, so that we may soften and even change our behaviors. Unlike Western psychology, which relies on the *Diagnostic and Statistical Manual of Mental Disorders (DSM)* to pathologize emotions neatly so that they fit into insurance billing codes, Buddhist psychology is based on the teachings of being in the present moment with love and compassion. It starts with the premise that our true nature is *sat-chit-ananda*, so we are naturally inclined to choose thoughts, words, and actions that move us toward happiness. When we are unhappy due to life circumstances of pain or loss of a loved one, Buddhist psychology encourages us to be present with our pain and suffering. We then find that living with equanimity is easier if we are living in the healing stream of love, compassion, and joy.

This may help us in working through our trauma by providing additional perspective on how we respond and react to our trauma in the first place. For example, when one person is faced with suffering, they might respond by dissociating or daydreaming to escape the situation. Another person might get anxious and have a fight response to the same situation. A third person may be comfortable sitting with the suffering and being compassionate toward themselves in the midst of their pain. Though research has not been performed to determine if and how the Buddhist personality types can assist with trauma healing, I have found it to be useful information so that I can customize mindfulness and trauma healing tools for my clients' unique needs.

While we are all some combination of the three Buddhist personality types, you can also determine which one dominates the way you live and which one is your greatest shadow that you try to avoid. Your personality type helps you cultivate a deeper understanding of the way your nervous system is wired to respond to life events. Identifying your Buddhist personality type is not about identifying your faults or pathologies; it is about understanding your own strengths and using them to move through your pain and suffering. Knowing the tendencies of your mind that can take you off course may be helpful for self-compassion and self-forgiveness—two essential elements of the healing journey. Remember, your Buddhist personality type is a lens that you should not take offense to. Your true nature is *sat-chit-ananda*, which is stress-free and blissful.

☸ Mindfulness Tool: Determining Your Buddhist Personality Type

Take this survey by circling the answers that most closely reflect how you view or respond to each situation. Keep in mind that if you feel like one or more of the answers in a category describe you, that is okay. Remember that we are all three personality types. Choose the answer that seems to reflect your thoughts or behaviors most often to determine your dominant personality. I encourage you to take the survey before reading ahead to the descriptions of the Buddhist personality type so that you won't be biased.

	My attitude toward	A	B	C
1	Cleanliness of my home	I thrive in clean and beautiful surroundings!	I can't stand clutter!	Despite my best efforts, my space gets a bit chaotic at times.
2	Running late	If I run late for something, it's probably because I was saying hello to friends or on the phone.	I'm particular about getting to places early and hardly ever run late.	I'm invariably running late because I can't find my car keys, my gym bag, or some other item I need.
3	Fitness class experience	During class, I find myself noticing how nicely someone is dressed, how fit they are, or how beautiful their yoga mat is.	During class, I am focused on what is being taught and make sure I do it correctly to not get injured.	During class, my mind wanders and sometimes I miss instructions.
4	Dining out	I like to eat delicious and beautifully prepared meals with wonderful companions in quality restaurants.	I like to eat perfectly prepared meals in a neat and clean environment where the service is immaculate.	My choice in restaurants depends on how I'm feeling that day, though often I'm perfectly fine letting someone else choose where we go.
5	Fashion	I like to be on-trend and am willing to invest in high-quality clothing that looks beautiful and makes a statement.	I am particular about keeping up with the trends, but if the current fashion doesn't suit me, then I don't bother with it.	I generally wear clothes that are comfortable. I can't really keep up with ever-changing fashion.
6	Home decor	My decor is aesthetically pleasing and very comfortable with well-matched, beautiful details.	My furniture is sturdy, practical, and will last a long time.	My decor choices are eclectic, balancing both investment pieces and thrift finds.

7	Vacationing	We enjoyed the art museum during the day, had an early dinner, and caught a Broadway play in the evening. The trip was more enjoyable due to our friends, who took us out on an evening cruise with live music.	We planned weeks ahead of time and it was perfect! We had reservations for five-star restaurants and purchased tickets ahead for the most popular Broadway show.	We stayed up so late and walked through the streets enjoying the parades. That night, I didn't sleep well. The next day, I ate leftovers and caught a red-eye back home. Overall, I had a great time.
8	Kitchen	I like to cook, so I have a chef-level stove and state-of-the-art gadgets.	I like to cook, and all my spice jars and gadgets are well labeled and stored correctly. Nothing unnecessary is in my kitchen.	I like to cook, and I usually throw together a dish. I wish I had more kitchen gadgets, but I make do with what I have.
9	Friends	I am friends with several people who are famous and popular on social media.	I am friends with people who are honest, upright, and engage in social projects.	I am friends with a variety of people from all walks of life.
10	Exercise	I have a regular exercise regimen and enjoy looking physically fit.	I have a regular exercise regimen so that I lower my risk for disease and other health conditions.	I try to keep a regular exercise regimen with a variety of exercises, but I am not consistent.
11	Social justice	I believe in opposing social injustices and have participated in protests along with my friends.	I support social justice causes because I cannot stand injustices inflicted on marginalized communities.	I support social justice causes. I can usually see both sides, but I usually stand in favor of causes that my friends and family believe in.
12	Work desk	My desk is clean with photos of my beloved and displays of all my awards.	My desk is clean and organized with folders of my projects, all neatly labeled.	I know exactly where things are in the midst of papers and files on my desk.

13	Work relationships and projects	My coworkers and my boss like me, and we often meet for lunch or drinks. My projects are generally on track.	My coworkers respect me due to the high quality of my work. My projects are on time and within budget.	My coworkers enjoy my company because I get along with everyone. I try my best to keep track of projects, though sometimes I have to work late to catch up on deadlines.
14	Work project going off track	I think, "This project will improve soon because I have such a great team."	I think, "Someone has made a critical error. Let me identify who it is and help them out."	I think, "I wonder if I have made a mistake in this project. Is this my fault?"
15	Managing stress	I try not to let stress get to me, so I usually have several plans in place to minimize my stress level throughout the day with friends, games, lunches, gym, music, dance, movies, meditation, etc.	I actively work at minimizing my stress, but being a perfectionist with high standards that others usually fall short of stresses me out. I manage my stress by creating daily routines such as exercise, meditation, hobbies, time with family and friends, etc.	I usually don't get stressed because I am easygoing and don't take things personally. However, I get stressed when I am unprepared and coming close to a deadline.
16	Intimacy and sex	I like to have soft sheets, candlelight, essential oils, and melodious jazz music when I am being intimate with someone. The mood and ambiance are important so that I can focus on my beloved.	I want my beloved to have a perfect evening so I carefully plan our date nights with wine, music, dinner, and entertainment that I am sure will meet my beloved's and my taste.	My beloved usually plans our date night, and I enjoy their company during the meals or entertainment. If it were up to me, our dates would be spontaneous and would most likely end in a disaster, albeit a fun one.

17	Money	I have a CPA friend who manages my finances. We meet every month to go over well-designed reports and review my finances.	My finances are well organized and easy to understand. I understand everything, and due to my keen attention to detail, I have found mistakes in tax returns prepared by my CPA.	I look at my finances periodically and it takes me some time to understand what they mean. Though I am not organized, I have a general idea about my finances.
18	Career areas	Among all the career choices, my current career is a perfect fit for my people skills and mental acuity.	I methodically arrived at my career. I took tests that identified my skillsets and selected the career best suited for me.	I did not plan on this career; I just happened to interview for this job and get it.
19	Responding to criticism	I hardly ever receive criticism. When I do, I usually offer a charming response that disarms the other person.	I am sensitive to criticism. I am a perfectionist, so when I am criticized, I question whether the other person really knows what they are talking about.	I hardly ever notice people criticizing me. When I do notice that I am being criticized, I overlook the harsh words, learn from the feedback, and continue about my ways.
20	Doctors	A doctor with good bedside manners is important to me.	My doctor's qualifications and experience are most important to me.	If the doctor has a degree, that's good enough for me.
21	Social media	I follow a diverse group of people who talk about fascinating topics.	I follow a select group of people who talk about topics relevant to my self-improvement.	I follow a diverse group of people I have found interesting in the past, but I don't really keep up with them now.
	Total			

Which area of the survey did you have the highest total for? If it was mostly As, your Buddhist personality is the Greed type. If you answered mostly Bs, you are an Aversive type. If you responded with mostly Cs, you are the Deluded type. Your highest number is your primary type. Then you have two subtypes. Your second-highest number is your secondary type. Your lowest number is your third type, or your shadow, which we will discuss at a higher level in the next chapter. In this chapter we will focus primarily on understanding your predominant personality type.

If these descriptions give you a bit of pause or feel off-putting, you are not alone. I struggled with my primary label, Deluded, and our modern social views of what being a deluded or delusional person means. Remember that in Buddhist psychology, these labels are meant to show you the color of the lens through which you are looking at the world while covering your true nature of *sat-chit-ananda*.

I do not want these labels to serve as a barrier to your healing process as they did mine. So, I have taken the artistic liberty of redefining each Buddhist personality type based on the strength of each one. If you're a Greed personality type, you can relabel yourself as the Optimist. If you're an Aversive type, you can relabel yourself as the Strategist. And if you're a Deluded type, you are the Peacemaker. Throughout the remainder of this chapter, I will refer to the personality types by both names (the original Buddhist name and my alternate label). You can choose to use whichever label you prefer.

Do not forget that we inhabit all three personality types. When you face a situation where you are unable to express your predominant Buddhist personality, you default to your second subtype. A new, challenging, or traumatic situation may elicit a response from your third subtype. As such, I would encourage you to read through each of the three types and not just skip to your dominant type. Having an understanding of the three personality types will also give you valuable insight into the behavior of other people in your life and why they respond in the ways they do—like the friend who always seems to want to control the restaurant you go to, the family member who hosts family gatherings differently from you, or the coworker who shuts down at even the smallest of criticisms. We can open our hearts and have a greater capacity for compassion for ourselves and others through understanding all three personality types.

The Greed or Optimist Type

While we all desire to be happy, the Optimist most actively seeks pleasant experiences to maintain balance in their mind and heart. Due to their ability to see the goodness and beauty in others and in life, the soaring strength of the human spirit amid the chaos of the sociopolitical environment, the Optimist type can be truly uplifting and inspiring to their coworkers, families, friends, and communities. In conversations with my Optimist friends, they are inspiring and energizing and will likely be the ones to point out the good or see the silver lining to difficult situations. They love to reframe unpleasant situations and may even gloss over them to avoid spending time focusing on problem areas. This can create challenges where issues go unaddressed because the Optimist tends to avoid the unpleasant.

Optimists can be found in people such as:

- A wonderful salesperson who truly believes in the quality of their product and enjoys sharing that information with others.
- A realtor who shows homes with enthusiasm and shares the highlights of the neighborhood.
- A business owner who speaks positively of their business, even in times of hardship.
- A teacher who uplifts their students' spirits and motivates them to try harder.

Optimist types are motivated by praise. This is a good framework to keep in mind if you're communicating with an Optimist. For example, if your boss fits this type, then it's best to give them status updates that start by stating everything that is going well. If your beloved is an Optimist and you're sharing how your day went, it is best to share your positive highlights first. Once an Optimist has received messages that are pleasing to them, they may become more empathetic to sad or stressful news.

This craving for pleasant experiences is both a benefit and a weakness for the Optimist type. In their work, they may prioritize projects and meetings that feel good to them, delaying or avoiding problem areas that need to be addressed in a timely manner. They may also be conflict avoidant, preferring to suppress words they need to share with another in favor of keeping the conversation positive. Optimists may have aesthetically beautiful homes with quality furniture and inviting design, but they may struggle with plumbing problems or a decaying frame because they avoid addressing the mundane and boring issues of life.

If you scored high in As and identified yourself as the Optimist type, then it is important that you are consciously aware of your tendency to gloss over the unpleasant. When it comes to healing trauma, you may be prone to spiritual bypassing or downplaying any feelings you have that could be perceived as negative. If you are able to patiently listen to others or surround yourself with friends who are not afraid to speak the truth, they can help balance this tendency, then your strength will carry you to heights beyond your wildest imagination.

Optimists may also find that they struggle with challenges of unhealthy habits or addiction. Because they are drawn toward the pleasant, this can result in things like overindulging or overspending. They will choose a second serving of ice cream over the second serving of broccoli, concerned less with their health and more with their short-term happiness. Staying with neutral or unpleasant flavors of experiences presents a real challenge for the Optimist.

An Optimist Story

Optimism is often a positive in life. It's a hopeful disposition that leads people to believe that life is good and will continue to get better. When it comes to trauma, however, the Optimist type may be inclined to skip over part of the healing process or attempt to fast-track their relief. Here is one such story about how an Optimist responded to healing from trauma.

My client Janna was a long-time meditator. Over the years, she participated in several long meditation retreats. On one of her retreats in July, she was sitting in silence when a firecracker went off outside her window. She was shocked at the sound, and her ears started ringing with tinnitus. No matter what she tried, the ringing wouldn't stop. The loud internal noise interfered with the silence of the retreat. As an Optimist type, Janna expected that the ringing would just go away, but it didn't. It persisted for weeks before she took action.

Janna came to me after returning home from her retreat. She could not understand why one firecracker could have triggered this event, particularly given that she typically enjoyed fireworks on the Fourth of July. I explained to her that this was likely a complex trauma, a layering of multiple past traumas, where the unexpected firecracker was simply the final jolt to the nervous system that sent her into this state. I reminded her that while we like to seek the "why" behind what happened, it was more important to focus on what was happening to her now. We had to shift her focus away from the event and toward healing her symptom.

Because of her Optimist personality, her mind was using all sorts of tricks to distract her from the unpleasant ringing. She would spend time asking herself questions like, "Why is this happening now when

I've never had an issue in past years?" When it came to talking through her trauma, she would crack jokes and make me laugh to lighten the mood and distract us from the heavy feelings.

It took compassion and patience for her to begin to sit with and address past traumas. As she did, however, the ringing lessened. This positive progress motivated her to continue her trauma healing work. Janna soon realized that through managing her level of stress, she could lessen the ringing noise. Within a month, she found improvement in her condition as the intensity of the ringing and her aversion to it steadily declined.

While none of us like staying with unpleasant experiences, Optimist types have the hardest time. For Optimist types to even acknowledge that they are suffering physically or psychologically, it often has to be severe enough to get in the way of them enjoying their daily life activities. It's only when their suffering reaches an extreme do the Optimist types finally seek help.

One of my friends, Liam, who is an Optimist type, started his inner work in his mid-fifties. With a lifetime's worth of traumatic experiences to process, he thought he could handle most of them within a few months, and then his pain would be over. In his therapy sessions, when things would start to get difficult, he would avoid the situation and instead seek a new therapist or a new healing modality. This allowed Liam to avoid going deeper into feelings he did not want to face. When he realized that this approach was not moving him toward his overall goal of healing, Liam finally started to become more patient with the speed of his healing journey and work consistently with his somatic therapist.

If an Optimist type walks into the office of a therapist, they probably have complex trauma that is interfering with their lives. The Optimist type doesn't like the unpalatable work of delving into the unpleasant, so working with small slices of suffering is highly recommended. During their trauma healing process, Optimists should take frequent breaks to focus on positive events in their lives. They need to carefully balance working on trauma in small pieces and then allowing time for rest. This gives them space to settle their nervous systems and feed their desire for the positive before returning to the difficult work.

☸ Mindfulness Tool: Working with Our Optimist Type

The work of the Optimist, when it comes to reigniting their power, is to become comfortable with the uncomfortable. Through practicing shifting into neutral and unpleasant experiences, the Optimist can build their resilience and dial back their "Good Vibes Only" mindset. Here is a practice to try.

1. Grab a notebook and something to write with. Begin by creating a list of positive or resourceful activities that you do that feel pleasant to you. This may be trying on new clothes, working in your garden, or eating a delicious meal.

2. Now create a list of unpleasant activities, things like cleaning a toilet, paying taxes, or arguing with a friend. Notice the unpleasant sensations in your body as you make this list.

3. See if your mind tries to move away from these sensations by giving you an entertaining thought, distracting you with a visual of something interesting in the room, or tempting you to grab your phone to scroll through social media. Name all the different ways you want to pull away from the unpleasant experience.

4. Pause for a few moments and connect with your breath.

5. Now, Choose Otherwise by incorporating a little more awareness of the discomfort of the unpleasant experience. To bring this exercise to a close, let go of observing the unpleasant and return to the pleasant experiences, allowing your nervous system to relax.

See how we just incorporated the Notice, Name, Pause, Choose Otherwise practice into our Buddhist personality types? If you are an Optimist type, do this exercise often to build your capacity to stay with the unpleasant experiences. If you are an Optimist, be aware of your tendency to shortcut your healing by declaring yourself "healed" prematurely. You deserve to be fully alive in that beautiful world that you are so drawn toward!

The Aversive or Strategist Type

Strategist types are the folks who have the capacity to see the unpleasant, to anticipate the unpleasant events, and to plan for these events. Their ability to critically evaluate, weigh options, and plan the best outcome is why I refer to them as the Strategist type. This Buddhist personality type looks to avoid risk. They find happiness by seeing what can potentially go wrong in a situation and relax by taking action to avoid mistakes or disasters. Unlike the Optimist, who only wants to see the good, the Strategist is looking for everything that *could* go wrong to prevent it from coming to fruition.

Strategist personality types have the ability to see all the different ways they can keep their loved ones and their communities safe, whether with well-placed signs on the highways, by plugging loopholes to minimize tax evasion, by designing car seats for kids, or through retrofitting historic homes in San Francisco with earthquake safety features. Strategist types have a sharp intellect and the essential critical thinking skills necessary for any walk of life. They are the protectors.

The Strategist type often struggles to accept praise for their accomplishments, seeing their role as one of necessity, not positive action. At the same time, they are highly motivated by avoiding mistakes and criticism. Most Strategists may not want the spotlight.

You will see Strategists in your life as:

- The neighbor who helps you prepare for a hurricane by sharing their sandbags, reminding you to fill your car with gas, or helping you trim tree branches that could potentially damage your property.

- The parent who is always pointing out what could go wrong or what you should be watching out for with any life choice you're making, from a new job to starting a family to renovating your home.

- The manager at work who starts projects by identifying the problem and its potential risks before sharing solutions and their recommended course of action.

- The meditation teacher who provides a critical analysis of a teaching by the Buddha, offers specific ways for the student to practice it, and warns against potential pitfalls along the path.

Due to their naturally discerning minds, Strategist types can see and stay with negative experiences. This can help them to work through challenging situations and difficult feelings; however, they may also struggle to shift into the positive of receiving praise or feeling better once the challenge has been avoided. If your boss is a Strategist type, it behooves you to start your project updates with all the problems that were identified and then mitigated. Doing so may help relax their nervous system, thus opening them up to hear what you're enjoying about the project or the accolades you are receiving for your good work. Similarly, when your Strategist type child comes home, allow them space to fill you in on all the things that went wrong before asking them what they enjoyed at school. After a few negative highlights, your child will be more open to remembering all the fun they had with their friends.

As with each of the Buddhist personality types, a Strategist's strength of focusing on risks can also be their weakness. They may be resistant to making changes to things purely for the aesthetic or enjoyment of the space. They are the neighbor who resists modernizing the paint color of their house because the expense doesn't provide a risk-preventing benefit. They are the politicians who may not be open to letting new industries enter the area because they do not feel fully briefed on what risks the new industry might create, or they have concerns about the industry's unproven stability and profitability. Strategists are the managers at work who hold their teams to an expectation of superior quality, potentially burning out the team with long work hours and minimal praise.

If you scored high in Bs and identified yourself as the Strategist type, your focus will be to bring balance to your critical but discerning mind so that you can achieve (and enjoy) greater success in all aspects of your life. Using the NNPCO tool, the Pause is essential for Strategist types because it creates space between their analysis of what could go wrong and their determination of how to accomplish the tasks, while supporting themselves and those around them. It is easy for the Strategist type to overwork in their zest to achieve perfection. But most times, what seems less than perfect for a Strategist type is beyond the expectations of most other people. For the overzealous Strategist, practicing the Choose Otherwise step may motivate them to select an option that may not meet their own expectation but still exceeds other's expectations.

Strategist types have an interesting conundrum when it comes to working with and healing from trauma. Due to their drive for seeking and correcting "broken" aspects of their lives, they can drive themselves too hard and not make time for rest, even when they need to. They may suffer from a strong inner critic, their inner voice that judges, criticizes, or belittles them and in turn drives them toward perfection at all times. Thus, in healing one area of their life, they can create problems in a different area.

A Strategist Story

My client Zuri knew from a young age that she did not want to adopt the mindset and behaviors of her parents. She was driven to create a different life from what she had grown up in and was highly aware of falling into her parents' dysfunctional ways of thinking and being. In her quest to push away her parental patterns within herself, she became quite successful in the business world, got married, bought her dream home with a white picket fence, and had a lovely little child. From the outside, it appeared that Zuri had successfully avoided recreating her parents' life.

As a Strategist type, Zuri showed tremendous psychological growth in her strong desire to avoid reliving her parental patterns. This aversion helped her grow significantly in her personal and professional life, but it also had a dark side. Her inner critic drove her to exhaustion and would not let her enjoy the life she had created. Zuri found herself suffering from depression and got a cancer diagnosis in her early thirties.

Since her work was a significant part of her identity, we had several conversations about the necessity for her to take medical leave. While on leave, she felt guilty for resting during her cancer treatments and couldn't give herself simple joys, like sitting in a coffee shop or enjoying the afternoon sun. Instead, Zuri took on home projects to feel productive. Then she would be physically drained and feel frustrated because she could not complete the project nor let go of the idea of leaving it incomplete. She sought mindfulness and somatic tools to help break out of her downward spiral of overwork, fatigue, and self-criticism.

The Strategist type has strengths that make them successful in their personal and professional lives, but their critical mind can also be their biggest saboteur. When this critical eye is turned toward themselves and others, they can pick faults and set expectations that can never be fully met. This wears down their personal and professional relationships, especially with people who report to them.

Strategists, like my client Zuri, may suffer from *high-functioning depression*, a term coined by Dr. Judith Joseph.[21] Unlike the common view of depression as a state where a person cannot find the motivation or energy to do things, Dr. Joseph describes high-functioning depression as pushing through and avoiding pain because you feel that too many people depend on you. Joseph says, "You know something's off, but you can't quite put your finger on it. And you don't slow down because you don't know how to."

While high-functioning depression is mostly absent from psychological literature, it describes the Strategist type well. The dedicated nature of the Strategist type is prone to overworking despite their mental and emotional state because they don't take their responsibilities lightly. It may be helpful for the Strategist type to seek exercises that help them slow down. They need practice saying "not now" when their inner drive pushes them to the next task or achievement. They need to build the capacity to leave things alone and rest in the midst of what may feel like chaos so that they can see that the world still turns without their intervention.

☸ Mindfulness Tool: Working with Our Strategist Type

The work of the Strategist, when it comes to reigniting their power, is to allow more pleasant and neutral experiences into their day. Through practicing shifting out of the unpleasant, the Strategist can give peace and calm to their overly taxed nervous system.

1. Grab a notebook and create a list of activities you don't enjoy.
2. As you imagine these activities (and later as you do them), feel the unpleasant sensations in your body. See if you can stay with

the unpleasantness of the sensation and not take any action.

3. Next, see if you can find some pleasant sensations and feel some relief. Imagine engaging in a pleasant activity and notice how your body and mind respond. If you are unable to find something pleasant, then do this step with a neutral activity.

We are building your capacity to stay with the unpleasant or things that need to be fixed and relax in the midst of them.

The Deluded or Peacemaker Type

In Buddhist psychology, the Peacemaker type are individuals who do not find themselves strongly drawn toward positive or negative experiences. Known for their balance and tendency to be more even-keeled, I refer to this type as the Peacemaker. Peacemakers are often steady and independent contributors who work long hours but with less burnout than the Strategist types. Peacemakers excel at seeing both sides of an argument and creating balanced solutions for the greater good.

The Peacemaker type is neutral in their nature, experiencing life with a slight flavor for the pleasant and a slight aversion to the unpleasant. They avoid extremes, thus keeping their senses from becoming overwhelmed. Due to this, they can have difficulty making decisions, choosing a side, or demonstrating discernment in what needs to be added or removed from situations. They see the purpose in all of it.

People are drawn to the Peacemaker because they make easygoing companions, often deferring to others with stronger emotions to decide where to go or what to do. Regardless of how things turn out, they'll often be satisfied. Peacemakers are quick to forgive others' mistakes and not hold grudges, often because words do not seem to cut them as deeply as they do with Optimists or Strategists.

Due to their ability to thrive on little, whether pleasant or unpleasant, they are self-motivated, self-directed, and not thrown off balance by blame or motivated by praise. Peacemakers are comfortable with chaotic or confusing situations, such as changes and transitions in relationships or work. They will not generally rush to find solutions and, instead, stay with the confusion and chaos until they determine what they consider to be the most reasonable solution. Often, issues resolve themselves without the Peacemaker having to take charge. This personality type is generally more easily able to access the heart energies of kindness, compassion, and forgiveness.

You will find Peacemaker types around you in:

- A friend who delays vacation plans to sit by the bedside of a friend who was moved into hospice care.
- A grandmother who loves both her grandchildren equally, even when other family members find an "unforgivable" fault in one of them.
- A project leader who reminds you of the lessons you've learned and growth opportunities from your failure on a project, drawing you away from self-criticism by reminding you of your strengths and past successes.
- A meditation teacher who imbues the room with a feeling of love and compassion and creates a space where you are able to forgive yourself for your weaknesses and remember that you are *sat-chit-ananda*, or truth, consciousness, and bliss.

When speaking to a Peacemaker type, you will find the beautiful benefit of having a space where you can openly speak your mind. Peacemakers will often receive information with acceptance and active listening. If, however, there is something that you need a Peacemaker to act urgently on, it is important to highlight that need or put a specific timeframe around it to ensure it catches their attention. Peacemaker types are often the contributors who can drive a project from start to finish with very little oversight from their managers. If the Peacemaker types are not focused on their path, they can deviate and get distracted. Conversely, if they have identified what they value in their work, they are likely to devote long hours without the need for outside motivation.

On the downside, the Peacemaker may come across as ungrounded, as their rationale for things may lack gravity or critical thinking. They may joyfully allow their beloved to make all the significant choices in their relationship until they realize what they actually enjoy and are drawn toward. At work, Peacemaker types may downplay successes and potential pitfalls in an effort to keep things moving forward at an even pace. This can be incredibly frustrating for Optimists or Strategists, who derive energy from these opposite ends of the spectrum.

Peacemaker types make excellent mediators due to their balanced nature but would struggle to be in a legal role where they could only argue for one side. They may appear as enablers, seeming to forgive behaviors without demanding change. They are the leaders who care more about the energy and happiness of their teams than the effectiveness of their work, sometimes leading to poor project management or performance. In meditation practices, I have seen them as teachers who would teach their students to open their hearts to love and compassion, but gloss over critical steps their students need to avoid potentially retraumatizing pitfalls.

If you scored high in Cs and identified yourself as the Peacemaker type, I encourage you to patiently wait to see which flavor is predominant in each experience: the pleasant or the unpleasant flavor. You may find that your mind wanders, as noticing the predominant flavor isn't important to you. If you are consistent and patient with yourself, then you will find that your discernment will emerge and strengthen. This will give your words gravitas, and your actions will be grounded in reality, which others will relate to more strongly. To stay consistent and on the path, I suggest Peacemaker types have a mentor, life coach, or a therapist to hold them accountable. When the mind of the Peacemaker can clarify in discerning between pleasant and unpleasant, they make tremendous progress in healing their traumas.

A Peacemaker Story

Mirroring is a process that happens during child development, where an adult (often a parent or caregiver) lovingly reflects back a child's thoughts, emotions, or behaviors to help recognize and make sense of them. Of the three Buddhist personalities, Peacemaker types most often lacked mirroring as a child to help them identify their desires and needs. Here is one example from my practice.

My client Saanvi found herself having to act independently from a young age due to abandonment and neglect from her parents. Saanvi's mother has severe depression, while her father was prone to unexpected outbursts of anger that kept everyone on edge. Due to this, Saanvi developed a high sensitivity to the needs of others, sensing people's emotions before they expressed them as a way to keep herself safe.

Due to her Peacemaker personality, many people around Saanvi leaned on her for emotional support and had no idea about the environment she grew up in. She got along well with almost everyone and was fun to be with; however, her internal confusion often left her blaming herself harshly in situations where she had not done anything wrong. This took its toll on Saanvi, who found herself regularly carrying the weight of other people's issues and allowing her own needs to go unmet.

Through our somatic trauma-healing work, Saanvi began to sit with her feelings so that she could untangle what belonged to her and what belonged to others. By staying with her pleasant and unpleasant experiences, she built the capacity to identify her needs and wants. As she did that, she learned that it was safe and okay to ask for what she needed and desired.

The Peacemaker type can stay calm and neutral when there are opposing views being voiced by others. But their external calm doesn't
always match their internal experience, which may feel disorganized
or chaotic. If the Peacemaker type can stay with their inner experience
and let it clarify into pleasant or unpleasant, that will help ground their
mind and lead them to inner growth.

Of the three personality types, Peacemakers are the most likely to
stay in unhealthy relationships for the longest time, due to their ability
to sustain themselves with little connection from their partner and
being out of touch with their own needs. This also applies to jobs. If
the Peacemaker type can clarify whether they are enjoying themselves
in a particular moment or not, that will help strengthen their ability to
notice when their needs are not being met and when it is time for them
to leave a relationship or a job.

☉ Mindfulness Tool: Working with Our Peacemaker Type

The work of the Peacemaker, when it comes to reigniting their power,
is to identify and strengthen both their pleasant and unpleasant experiences. Optimist and Strategist types will benefit from this exercise as
well because it will help relax their nervous systems. However, they are
likely to find the exercise boring or may feel sleepy.

1. Set a timer for one minute and look at the color of the wall
   nearest you. The more neutral or plain the wall, the better. If
   you're in a space with wallpaper or artwork, I suggest moving to
   a different location.

2. Look at the wall for the full minute, paying attention to your
   thoughts and how your body feels. Notice if you find the neutral
   color to be soothing or not. Notice if your body relaxes in any

way, such as by taking a deep breath or increasing the amount of saliva in your mouth.

3. After the minute is up, determine if your thoughts allowed you to stay present in the neutral state, if they drifted into positive experiences, or if they left you feeling agitated or frustrated.

4. If you've moved out of neutral, take a moment to notice and name what you are feeling.

This is an important exercise in allowing yourself to move out of neutral and recognize your feelings, whether pleasant or unpleasant. Give yourself a chance to feel them and give them permission to exist.

Using Your Buddhist Personality Type for Healing

Whether you identify with Optimist, Strategist, or Peacemaker, your personality type is key to understanding yourself better. Now that you've identified your primary Buddhist personality type and understand your other subtypes, you have a greater awareness of the types of experiences you gravitate toward and shy away from. In the next chapter we'll discover methods to use this knowledge in your trauma healing process.

Remember that there is no personality type that is better than the others when it comes to healing; they all have their own separate journey with their own strengths and challenges. However, I hope this awareness will support you in deepening your self-compassion as you work through difficult emotions, memories, and experiences. When you understand the lens you're using to view the world, you've taken an important first step in moving toward accessing your true nature of *sat-chit-ananda*, where you are happy, blissful, and stress-free.

The Buddhist Personality Types and Trauma

*To be beautiful means to be yourself. You don't need to be accepted
by others. You need to accept yourself.*

—Thich Nhat Hanh

Buddhist psychology is a system that dates back approximately 2,500 years, yet its lessons and applicability carry through to our modern lives. The personality types help provide us with useful insights to understand our behaviors, reactions, strengths, and barriers in moving through life. At the same time, they are merely a lens through which to see ourselves and others.

When the personality types were initially presented in the *Visuddhimagga*, they were a commentary on how a teacher should give instructions to their meditation students to suit the temperament of each person. The intention was not to create a system to justify self-judgment or loathing. Instead, the personality types highlight why we all have different needs and desires in how we communicate, how we move through life, and how we heal. In this chapter, I share my own findings about how the Buddhist personality types can be useful based on conversations with my clients and Jungian psychology. Hold the information in this chapter loosely as a gentle guide to help you move toward greater awareness in each area of your life.

✿ Mindfulness Tool: The Wheel and Your Buddhist Personality Type

Look back at chapter one and the Your Resiliency Wheel Mindfulness Tool you completed when you first started on your journey. Let's take a fresh approach to it with the new knowledge of our Buddhist personality types. Ask yourself:

- Which areas of my life am I succeeding in due to my primary Buddhist personality type?
- Which areas of my life are more challenging due to my primary Buddhist personality type?

Now, consider the Buddhist personality type that ranked lowest for you (your third type) and ask yourself:

- Is my third personality type making these challenging areas more difficult?

We will discuss more about the third personality type in this chapter, but know for now that often your third type represents your shadow self, or the aspects of your personality that you keep hidden from yourself and the world.

Before we continue, consider where you started on your Resiliency Scale in chapter 1 and reassess yourself now. Has your number shifted?

How Trauma Gets Enhanced by Our Buddhist Personality Type

Our Buddhist personality types are almost as unique to us as our fingerprints or the iris of our eyes. Based on your scores from the Determining Your Buddhist Personality Type exercise in the previous chapter, we are now ready to explore your full profile. The highest score is your strength and your default mode of operation, second highest score is your next strength, and lowest score is your third personality type. Based on the three personality types, there are six possible combinations:

- Optimist-Strategist-Peacemaker
- Optimist-Peacemaker-Strategist
- Strategist-Optimist-Peacemaker
- Strategist-Peacemaker-Optimist
- Peacemaker-Optimist-Strategist
- Peacemaker-Strategist-Optimist

Within these six combinations, the weight of each personality type is different for each individual. Even among people with the same personality type layering, one might be 45% Optimist, 30% Strategist, and 25% Peacemaker, while another person is 65% Optimist, 30% Strategist, and 5% Peacemaker. This is why we must exercise caution when projecting on others what we assume their personality types to be, particularly if we believe that someone else has a similar personality type to us and thus could heal from trauma using the same methods that worked for us. This information can help us to be more compassionate toward others but should not become prescriptive in how we assume they should help themselves. Reflect back on your scores and see which of these combinations matches your Buddhist personality type.

Our Buddhist personality types, and how they are layered, can give us important insights into healing our own trauma. Take, for example, my client Amor.

Amor's primary Buddhist personality type was the Optimist, someone strongly drawn toward pleasant-flavored experiences. When Amor came to me, he was a single father whose children had grown and left home. He had also recently retired from his job. Amor found himself with a tremendous amount of free time, which he didn't know how to fill. The emptiness felt uncomfortable, and he unsuccessfully tried to fill the space with things like buying a new sports car and trying online dating. This time in Amor's life felt incredibly confusing as he now found the majority of his life experiences to be of a neutral flavor. Amor's work was to get comfortable with the neutral feeling of being an empty nester with a lot of free time, while also discovering new experiences that were fulfilling to him instead of simply chasing excitement.

In addition to our most dominant personality type, we should remain aware of our third, nondominant personality type. Swiss psychologist and psychiatrist Carl Jung would likely have referred to this third personality type as one's *shadow self*.[22] Our shadows—the third personality type—are the unfamiliar aspects of our personality that we must consciously work on. Without an awareness of our shadow, we can sometimes feel blindsided by trauma when it occurs in our third personality type. Because our shadow is not an aspect of ourselves that we've consciously dealt with, we often lack the tools to process the trauma. This may enhance our pain and confusion. For example, if someone has a third personality type of a Peacemaker and their trauma brings up a freeze response, then it will be difficult for them to deal with the confusion and dissociation from the freeze and their Peacemaker personality. They will need someone to guide them out of their trauma.

In the next section, I will share client stories and additional insights on each of the six combinations of the Buddhist personality types. Remember these combinations are based on the scores you received in the personality test in the previous chapter. I realize that the personality combinations may feel like a lot of information. I recommend that you start by skipping to your combination first. Learn to understand yourself through this context. When you feel ready, you can return and read the other personality types at a later time. They may give insight into others in your life and the unique ways that they move through the world.

The Optimist-Strategist-Peacemaker

Sofia learned from a very young age to read others' emotions and to put on whatever face they wanted to see. This often meant acting happy and not sharing other emotions. When Sofia experienced childhood sexual abuse, she hid it from her family so as not to make them feel guilty for neglecting her safety.

As an adult, her attunement to the emotions of others made her a highly sought-after therapist. She spent most of her time attending to the needs of others and was loved in her community for it. At the same time, she struggled to receive care from others. When a friend threw her a birthday ceremony to celebrate her, she stated that she would only participate in the ceremony if her other fifteen friends agreed to take care of themselves during that time. She was concerned that if they didn't agree to their own care, then they would be expecting her to tend to their needs instead of her own. She did not want to feel that anyone would hold her lack of care toward her friends against her.

During the ceremony, Sofia became aware of a sensation in her face, like a cold aloofness under her skin. She felt an aversion to it, which sent her into her Peacemaker (Deluded) shadow self. In it, Sofia felt her reality flip, with the sudden feeling that she couldn't tell whether her friends and family loved her and cared about her. She felt unsafe and wanted everyone to leave her alone in the midst of the ceremony.

Rather than run from the discomfort though, Sofia paused and stayed with her own confusion. The confusion began to transform, with Sofia shifting back into feeling solid, protected, and at home.

The skin on her face shifted from the aversive feel of aloofness to a new sensation of thinness, like the petals of a flower. Her "thick skin" that she had developed from her childhood to shield her true emotions from everyone was beginning to fade. She felt the new ability to wear her true emotions on her face. She was struck by a strong feeling that she was born for love!

As the ceremony concluded, Sofia went up to each friend, held their hands, looked into their eyes, and said, "I was born to love you!" Many of her friends melted into tears from this feeling of love and connection, and Sofia realized that she was loved and cared for by her friends. Sofia began to heal from her childhood trauma, realizing that she was safe and could be seen and accepted for who she was, not who she pretended to be.

Working With Our Optimist-Strategist-Peacemaker Personality

For an Optimist with a Peacemaker personality as their shadow, it can be challenging to sit with strong aversive feelings and memories. Sofia's childhood trauma and shadow aspect were not suddenly healed thanks to one thoughtful ceremony. Instead, she found herself slipping back into states of confusion where she could not tell if her friends truly loved and cared for her. She struggled to make sense of her feelings because they had never been mirrored back to her as a child. This lack of knowledge triggered her feelings of self-worth. The ceremony had activated Sofia's third personality type, which was unknown territory to her. Formerly confident (or appearing confident) in her life, Sofia now found herself saying, "I don't know" as confusion spread to other areas of her life.

Remember that the Peacemaker is not strongly drawn to pleasant or unpleasant flavors of experiences and sometimes lacks the ability to discern what it is that they feel toward things. If the Peacemaker is your third personality, it will likely feel incredibly uncomfortable to sit in these feelings of not knowing. Our work becomes a practice of staying with the not knowing. Like the exercise of staring at the neutral wall, it is likely that if we can pause long enough, our not knowing will shift into a pattern where we feel more clarity. Sofia realized that in pausing, she could eventually get in touch with her underlying emotions, though it was a slow and tedious process.

If you are struggling to pause in the feeling of not-knowing, offer yourself compassion and permission to surrender to the unfolding of your inner process. It is likely that your second type, the Strategist, will be unavailable to you to rationalize or create solutions. Allowing your Peacemaker to step out of the shadow will eventually allow you greater capacity to feel emotions like grief, loss, and sadness, which your Optimist personality attempted to hide from you. Having access to the full spectrum of emotions may allow you to unfold new life pathways.

For Sofia, this meant learning to exercise patience and sit with the slow and confusing nature of her trauma. Her Optimist desire to only feel good things had to cede to her Peacemaker. Eventually, with patience and self-compassion, Sofia's trauma from masking her feelings could resolve as she got in touch with her true needs and desires.

The Optimist-Peacemaker-Strategist

Dee was primarily an Optimist, and her shadow personality type was that of the Strategist. She was full of positive energy and gravitated toward the pleasant flavor of experiences, while being quite averse to anything with an unpleasant flavor. Interestingly enough, Dee took a job that was very detail-oriented and number-based, a field that typically attracts Strategist types. Dee often found that she would blank out or dissociate while working, triggering her Peacemaker (or Deluded) personality type. Then she would not be able to tap her Strategist to go back and verify the quality of her projects. This expended a tremendous amount of Dee's energy and made her feel miserable about her career as her work was riddled with errors.

Dee was also prone to being in the nervous system state of freeze due to unresolved childhood trauma. As an adult, she began working with me to somatically bring more awareness to the sensations in her body. She also began practicing yoga and stretching daily in an attempt to increase her body awareness and move out of freeze. While her job activated her Peacemaker personality, sending her into a state of not-knowing, her bodywork exercises brought her back into sensations she could clearly define as something she liked or disliked. She slowly developed her Strategist and learnt to double- or triple-check her work to make sure she completed it correctly. As her performance improved and she relaxed, she realized she was in the wrong job and relationship and made changes in both areas of her life.

Working with Our Optimist-Peacemaker-Strategist Personality

People with this layering of the Optimist Buddhist personality type often do what they can to stay in feelings of positive energy, and avoid feelings associated with pain or trauma at all costs. As I mentioned in the previous chapter, individuals prone to spiritual bypassing may fit this personality type. They desire to do the work in ways that feel pleasant to them rather than facing anything that might feel unpleasant. This may lead to constantly being in a cycle of healing at more superficial levels without addressing the deeper trauma that is causing their pain.

Because this personality type lacks the discernment abilities of the Strategist type, I have found that starting with modalities that address body sensations and feelings of pain or tightness are most effective. This way, the person can get used to staying with unpleasant physical sensations. Slowly, they may be able to stay with their unpleasant emotions that are part of their fight, flight, or freeze response. People with this Buddhist personality type may not tolerate working directly with their trauma due to the intensity of the unpleasant sensation. It will feel overwhelming because their Strategist isn't developed and their Peacemaker may lead them to dissociate. Instead, a more gradual approach to healing is recommended.

The Peacemaker-Strategist-Optimist

Maia lived on the East Coast and was preparing to take her LSAT exams for entrance into law school. After an unexpected whirlwind romance, she fell in love with a young, handsome entrepreneur who had just received funding to launch his startup in Silicon Valley. Being a predominant Peacemaker, she was easily swept off her feet and agreed to move with him to San Francisco and continue her preparations there.

While her Strategist function would have made a good lawyer and her Peacemaker function had the patience and perseverance to study for law school, she did not take into consideration the distractions and the impact of being in a new environment. Her preparations started to falter and her practice test scores started to decline. Her new boyfriend was in his element in the Bay Area and wanted to socialize with potential clients, but Maia was now confronted with her Optimist (Greed) shadow. She could not find the joy in meeting new people because her LSAT preparations were not up to par.

The Strategist in her would be overly critical of herself, her beloved, and her new environment. Try as she might, she could not relax and enjoy her life and found herself in a spiral of dissociation and high stress. This was not a good combination and soon Maia realized that she would score so low on her LSAT that she would not be able to enter a law school. Seeing her dream turn to ashes, she decided to leave her beloved and return to the East Coast.

When Maia came to see me, one of the first skills we worked on was taking in the simple pleasures of life to strengthen the Optimist within her. She worked patiently and was soon able to take in joy every hour. We also worked on finding ways to lessen her procrastination due to her Peacemaker function. She started planning her day, and, with good time management, she was less critical of herself. Her stress level decreased and so did her stress-induced dissociation. Once she was able to access the rest and relaxation of her Optimist, she was able to turn on her parasympathetic nervous system and was able to study and retain information. Soon Maia's practice scores for LSAT improved, and she confidently aced her tests and received admission in a law school of her choice.

———————

Of all of the personality type combinations, this is one that I come across the least. The disparity between the Peacemaker's challenge of discernment and the Strategist's strength of knowing what to do next seems to put these personalities at odds with themselves. They may have moments of feeling decisive, but then often fall back into confusion, apathy, or regret toward their choices. They can also find themselves in the depths of detail-oriented study of ways to heal their trauma, but then fall into self-criticism and become critical of the process itself and abandon it.

One of the most significant difficulties for the Peacemaker-Strategist-Optimist type when it comes to healing trauma is finding resources that feel good to them and work for them. Resources are essential for the nervous system to relax and access the healing abilities of the parasympathetic response. Due to the Peacemaker's challenge in knowing what they need, finding a resource that seems like a good fit may be a challenge. Their Strategist personality may lead them to self-sabotage if they pick a technique or modality that isn't "serious" enough or doesn't seem to produce results fast enough. The Peacemaker personality may then get fatigued from trying to find the right option, instead choosing to simply tolerate whatever is not working in their lives.

Working with Our Peacemaker-Strategist-Optimist Personality

If you are of this personality type, my suggestion would be to identify three different resources that may assist you in your healing. When you notice negative self-talk arise, remind yourself of the benefits of the resources you chose. Give yourself a timeframe to commit to each of the resources and notice the flavor of your experiences with the resources.

Most importantly, show yourself compassion with the understanding that your Optimist type is your shadow. Slowly work to integrate stronger pleasant flavors into your life, knowing that they don't always have to solve a problem or have a purpose. Learning to discern what you like and permitting yourself to enjoy them without your Strategist's logic or approval is a valuable part of your healing journey.

The Peacemaker-Optimist-Strategist

Ellen found herself repeating the pattern of staying in unhealthy relationships throughout her life. From childhood, she would cling to one-sided friendships or unrequited love interests due to her Peacemaker personality type. As a Peacemaker, Ellen had neither a strong pull toward nor a strong aversion to the pleasant and unpleasant in life. Her ability to see both sides of things made her incredibly patient with people, often beyond the point that was healthy for her.

As an adult, Ellen found herself in a traumatic relationship with a partner who experienced bipolar disorder. He originally swept her off her feet, quitting his job as a professor to move closer to her so that they could date. She held onto memories of this initial sacrifice as evidence that he loved her, even though his frequent violent outbursts sent her nervous system into a state of freeze. The quality of the Peacemaker type is that they do not need strong positive or negative reinforcement to stay with something or leave it behind. Instead, they will continue steadily working on things in their life, even if they see little improvement.

Due to Ellen's Peacemaker personality type, we realized that it would be difficult and time-consuming to directly address her freeze response, as she was unsure of her own feelings and desires. Instead, we worked on strengthening her Optimist and Strategist functions by doing exercises that allowed her to practice clearly defining what she liked and disliked. She used her Peacemaker strengths of patience, persistence, and perseverance to stay with these exercises until she built more trust in her body and emotions to guide her toward her authentic desires. As Ellen came out of her freeze response and shifted down the trauma response ladder into a fight and flight response, she took up running and kickboxing to expend the nervous system energy her body was trying to release.

Working with Our Peacemaker-Optimist-Strategist Personality

The Peacemaker type needs support to stay on course during their healing process. Once Ellen understood her personality type, she used her strengths to support her trauma healing work. Additionally, her awareness of the challenges of her Buddhist personality type allowed her to approach her trauma in a way that wouldn't potentially send her deeper into freeze.

A combination of freeze dissociation and Peacemaker as the primary personality type means that the healing process is slow and time-consuming. Patience and perseverance are required to move the nervous system back within the window of tolerance. It is helpful for Peacemakers to do their healing work with the support of someone who possesses fine observation skills and can reflect progress in the Peacemaker's healing to keep them motivated and accountable.

The Strategist-Peacemaker-Optimist

Rose came from an immigrant family that moved more than fifteen times in her youth. As a result, she found herself unable to make friends in school or feel like she could put down roots. In each location, her family struggled to assimilate as they did not speak English well and avoided socializing with their neighbors.

In adulthood, Rose's Strategist figured out the core cause of her rootlessness and anxiety, and she became committed to finding the stability that she lacked growing up. She found an apartment in the city and took a job as a paralegal. Unfortunately, her boss was verbally abusive. Her nervous system response activated her Peacemaker personality type, and she found herself disconnecting and daydreaming to mentally escape her work environment. The quality of her work suffered, prompting more verbal abuse from her boss. Her Strategist was self-critical and judgmental of her poor-quality work, which added to her overall stress.

Due to her upbringing, she was not willing to move jobs and start afresh in a new work environment. Her nervous system had moved from fight or flight and into freeze in her Peacemaker personality type. Rose had to regain her sense of safety to move out of freeze, but she was unable to access her Optimist personality type. She was unable to relax and find joy in her life. She needed the Optimist to break the cycle of self-critical Strategist and the overwhelmed, escapist Peacemaker. She came into my private practice, and we worked on her ability to sit and tolerate her Strategist-aversive feelings. Slowly she realized that she disliked her current job.

Her Strategist personality took action to move past her fear of moving, and she started searching for a new job. We also developed her Optimist by finding joy in the little things of life. She learnt to stop and figuratively smell the roses by doing things she enjoyed but had not previously made time for, like riding her bike on trails, exploring museums, and just going out for fresh air in the midst of her workday. As we strengthened her Optimist, she was able to identify a new position in a healthier environment, and her new boss mentored her toward success.

Working with Our Strategist-Peacemaker-Optimist Personality

It's not uncommon for this personality type to try and overwork their way to a solution. The Strategist in them is prone to being a workaholic, while their inner Peacemaker encourages them to stay the course regardless of the obstacles they encounter or how effectively they're reaching their goals. Like Rose, if they choose a course and stay with it due to unresolved trauma, they will likely stay in dysfunctional relationships or jobs for a long time without intervention.

If this is your personality type, your edge is to practice taking breaks from work and finding pleasurable activities that don't have a purpose or output besides sheer enjoyment and develop your Optimist. This presents a real challenge to most Strategist-Peacemaker-Optimists because they are least motivated by the pleasant flavor of experiences as that quality resides within the Optimist personality type—their shadow—and they don't have access to it. Besides, their Strategist may be self-critical and judgmental for spending useless time doing things they enjoy. The Optimist activity of having fun in their daily life is an essential part of their healing process. Finding relaxing activities is essential for them as it helps build their resources and activates their parasympathetic response, which is essential for balancing their nervous system. Strengthening the Optimist within them will guide them toward making fulfilling choices in life.

The Strategist-Optimist-Peacemaker

Ji-hye was a computer scientist in Seoul, South Korea, when she learned yoga from a famous teacher and realized that was her path. She immediately started studying under this teacher and did not think twice about spending more than $40,000 on her education in yoga, Qigong, and meditation. She had found her life path, and she quit her day job in the business world to become a full-time yoga instructor. Ji-hye moved to the U.S. to volunteer as a teacher at the centers owned by her Korean teacher.

Due to her sharp and critical mind as a Strategist, she became the director of the center, though her work was still mostly unpaid. In addition to teaching multiple classes, offering healing sessions, and providing counseling every day, she was in charge of scheduling, greeting the students and parents of the kids, and managing the finances of the center. She was deeply fulfilled by the teachings and the benefit to the students, which allowed her Peacemaker to gloss over the financial red flags she witnessed at the healing center. While Ji-hye was making significant contributions to the center, the Korean teacher was the only one who benefited financially and became famous due to the hard work of Ji-hye and other employees.

There came a point when Ji-hye's body gave way to burnout and immense fatigue. She left the center and sought healing. When Western medicine wasn't able to heal her, she decided to heal herself in the Taoist method by increasing and strengthening the energy circulation within her body. Ji-hye chose a unique way to work with her health challenge by learning Taekwondo and eventually earning her black belt. It was a long process that was a testimonial to her grit, patience, and perseverance—all qualities of the Peacemaker.

As she rebuilt her body, she added Korean martial arts, kickboxing, and Muay Thai to her exercise routine. Her philosophy is to incrementally keep growing. She shared, "If you are sick and ill now, then take some rest but find some exercise that you can do two or three times a week. Then increase the amount to six days a week. I like to have one day off to rest my body. If you cannot exercise, then walk. If you can walk, then walk faster. If you can walk faster, then run. You can take a break when you are tired. But never stop. Once you make a habit, you can do anything."

Now, the Strategist in Ji-hye teaches yoga classes multiple times a week to the older students who followed her from the Korean teacher's yoga center. She created community with a tea ceremony after each yoga class where she serves tea to her students, including one who is one hundred years old.

This personality type pairs what may feel like opposite ends of the spectrum: strong motivation due to unpleasant flavors, followed by strong motivation for pleasant flavors. With the ambivalent Peacemaker in the third position, this personality type is most likely to address and work through their trauma quickly and effectively. They do not have an aversion to sitting with difficult feelings and spend their energy seeking practical solutions. If things become too much for their nervous system, they may actually shift into their Optimist personality type, avoiding overwork or negativity by favoring things that feel good.

The Strategist function supports them in discerning the best path forward in their healing process. The Optimist function can help them identify and enjoy their resources as well as rest and recharge by moving their Parasympathetic nervous system to further tackle the next level of traumatic memories. If they can manage their Peacemaker in the shadow function and stay consistent in their healing process, then they will progress in their healing fairly quickly.

Working with Our Strategist-Optimist-Peacemaker Personality

If this is your personality type, you likely feel ready to sit with your trauma. Difficult feelings do not scare you in the way that they do with other personalities. It is likely that you've researched your type of trauma and have looked into solutions that help you face it, including the benefits of holistic methods like mindfulness and somatic therapies.

Use your personality type to create an awareness that while you're comfortable with discomfort, toiling through the unpleasant experiences is not your only road to healing. Work at identifying what experiences are pleasant to you as well, and allow yourself, with permission and compassion, to rest and enjoy things that feel good to you.

Your Unique Healing

I hope that this understanding of your Buddhist personality type is helping you shift into a greater sense of self-compassion and understanding of why not all healing modalities work the same for everyone. There is a beauty in us discovering our own unique journeys, but also the challenge in knowing that the answers are not always easy.

There is one thing we all have in common, though. Enhancing our ability to discern the pleasant, unpleasant, and neutral flavors in our lives; observing how we react to them; and showing ourselves love and kindness in working with them will thin the lens through which we see the world and move us closer to our *sat-chit-ananda*.

We are all love incarnate. In part three, I will guide you through practices of the heart and how they relate to our healing from trauma. We will maintain our mindfulness of our Buddhist personality types and use them as a tool to further understand how they play a role in the areas of tenderness and benevolence, joy and delight, and gratitude and forgiveness, culminating in a sense of balance. You deserve love, kindness, and care from others in your life, but most especially yourself.

PART THREE

Heart Practices for Releasing Trauma and Reigniting Your Power

Loving-Kindness

When you get to a place where you understand that love and belonging, your worthiness, is a birthright and not something you have to earn, anything is possible.

—Brené Brown

What is the goal of healing our trauma? The answer is likely different for everyone, but all may be rooted in the desire to reclaim our power and our resilience. As we release our trauma, we regain our lost sense of self-worth, love, and inner beauty. Our heart is able to trust and love people and life itself. We are curious, alive, and resilient as we were as children. This beautiful life has certain qualities of mind and heart that are called the Four Sublime States, or Divine Abodes, in Buddhism. It is interesting that when we consciously tend to the garden of our heart, these qualities of heart and mind naturally arise and help us heal and let go of our past trauma.

In this final part of the book, we'll be exploring these Four Sublime States of being: loving-kindness, compassion, joy, equanimity, and the unsung Sublime States of gratitude and forgiveness. Imagine feeling love, happiness, community, and peace in your healing journey instead of loneliness, isolation, and despair. It is possible when these Sublime States consciously become part of your day-to-day life! We all experience these states throughout the day because these Sublime States surround us all the time. It's just that we are not conscious of them.

Just as we don't see the oxygen in the air we breathe, we imbue these Sublime States without our conscious realization, and they nourish and balance us. In this way, the power of loving-kindness, compassion, joy, and equanimity reignite our internal power, returning us to *sat-chit-ananda*—our true nature. From this space, we can live as we are truly meant to.

In this chapter, you will learn about becoming aware of them when they arise and partaking of them consciously, just as you drink water when you are thirsty. By inhabiting your true nature with these Sublime States, your limitless love not only benefits you but also all beings around you. What is fascinating about Buddhism is that it also identifies the dark side of these Sublime States. We will explore the *near enemies*, or emotions that resemble these Sublime States, and *far enemies*, or the states that are the opposite of these Sublime States.

Though "enemy" may sound like a strong word to you, I encourage you to keep an open mind, as these enemies are the qualities that can act as barriers to healing your heart. The far enemies are the direct opposite of the Four Sublime States: hatred, cruelty, envy, and greed. They are easier to identify and, thus, may be easier to distance yourself from.

More challenging are the near enemies, which may seem similar to the beautiful states that you are trying to develop but are actually obstacles. They are attachment, pity, comparison or hypocrisy, and indifference. All these emotions close our heart and keep us stuck in a small and closed off space of trauma.

My wish is that you not judge yourself when these emotions arise. Your mindful awareness of them is sufficient to hold space for them and to release them. We all face our near and far enemies throughout our lives. After all, we are only humans who have bravely undertaken this epic journey of healing our trauma!

Understanding Loving-Kindness

Loving-kindness is more than an emotional state of being; it is a way of existing with the sincere wish for the well-being, happiness, and safety of all beings, including oneself. To experience loving-kindness means to cultivate a boundless and unconditional love that transcends personal biases or boundaries. When we are in a state of loving-kindness, we are able to express it with everyone around us, regardless of our past relationships, hurts, or challenges.

In one sense, love is so difficult to describe, yet we've known exactly what it is since we were babies. Instinctively, babies quiet down when held with love and cry if the person holding them is stressed, irritated, or impatient. Animals, like dogs and horses, come closer to strangers who exude a vibration of love. There are stories of people doing loving-kindness meditation in the forests and wild animals like tigers, elephants, birds, and snakes coming close to the meditators without harming them. Animals are very perceptive to energetic states.

Love is a heart vibration of harmony, peace, curiosity, and well-being. When you are in the space of love, you are so full of wonder that you wish good things would happen to others and you wish them well. The English language is limited in that it has just one word for love, whereas the Indian languages of Sanskrit and Hindi have several words to describe it.

The love I want to describe is called *maitri* in Sanskrit or *metta* in Pali. There is no English word to capture the essence of this state so it is loosely translated to "loving-kindness." When I first heard the English phrase "loving-kindness," I could not imagine this feeling and wasn't sure that I had ever felt it in my entire life. But, when I looked at loving-kindness more closely, I could feel it was an open-hearted vibration. It was expansive and without borders.

One way I love to describe loving-kindness is that it's a feeling where you are flowing in a stream of love and can't differentiate yourself from the stream. Perhaps you've felt this stream feeling when you're at a baseball game and your team hits a home run. The entire stadium erupts into cheers as one. You may have felt the feeling of the stream at a comedy show where the entire audience is caught up in laughter, or at a concert where the crowd rhythmically sways with the music. I had this feeling of being part of the stream while at a meditation retreat listening to an inspiring talk on Dharma and finding myself falling in love with Dharma as if for the first time.

When you are in a large crowd of like-minded people, you experience this feeling of being in a stream of emotion that carries you beyond your usual boundaries. The feeling of loving-kindness has a similar quality. Your heart is so open that well-wishes flow from you. This open-hearted feeling is not just that your physical heart is open, but your emotional and spiritual hearts are also open. You can't locate these anatomically, but they are in the center of your chest so when they are open, there is a feeling of physical expansion in that area. It's as if your hands are raised in blessing and you would offer everything that is good to the person before you, whether they are your loved ones, friends, strangers, or people you hold a grudge against, along with all the beings with whom you share this beautiful blue planet like plants, animals, birds, insects, fishes, and mammals.

Loving-kindness gives us the capacity to show up as we desire, even in challenging situations. Years ago, I had the pleasure of meeting Premvarni, a renowned meditation teacher whose primary focus was on teaching love and loving-kindness. His messages were so impactful that he attracted people from around the world, including members of the Beatles, to his ashram in India. As awareness of Premvarni's teachings grew, so did the crowds that flocked to his small town in the foothills of the Himalayas.

One evening, two thieves came to rob Premvarni's beloved property. As Premvarni was checking his property, the thieves stabbed him in the head with a *kukri*, a double-edged knife, and left him for dead.

Premvarni entered *samadhi*, or a deep meditative state, as he lay on the ground profusely bleeding through the night.

When he was discovered in the morning and rushed to the hospital to be operated on, they discovered that a piece of his skull bone was missing. Premvarni believes that one of the many coyotes on this property may have taken the piece, as it was never recovered. Premvarni's road to healing was challenging, with his open skull being affected by the slightest changes in temperature and atmospheric pressure. These sensations brought about severe and sudden changes in his mental and emotional states.

Premvarni leaned into his teachings and always tried to return to a space of love to harmonize his brain. When I met him, he would not only offer teachings and meditations, but he also cooked the most delicious food and chai. He said that he added his secret ingredient of love to everything he cooked. I found myself easily filled with profound love and kindness in his presence.

One day, Premvarni spoke harshly to me in a way that felt out of character with the loving being that I had enjoyed being around. While I understood that the change in personality was likely due to his skull injury, the exchange still hurt my feelings. I am human, after all. Later that day, Premvarni called me aside and apologized. He explained that his wound made him feel like an injured lion that occasionally lashes out in defense. As we were both in a state of loving-kindness, I was able to understand and not hold his words against him. I am glad we kept our relationship alive because the daily love and support he gave me during my darkest hours was deeply nurturing and healing.

While loving-kindness is a boundless expression of love, there are also times where we need to set boundaries or make choices that protect our peace. It's important to understand that we can both have loving-kindness for everyone around us and still choose to engage in relationships with healthy boundaries. Author Prentis Hemphill's often-cited quote is, "Boundaries are the distance at which I can love you and me simultaneously."[23]

One example of a relationship that involved both loving-kindness, a trauma response, and boundaries is the story of my client, Nash.

As a child, Nash did everything he could to please his father. His love for his father was boundless, even if the relationship between the two was dysfunctional and left Nash with layers of childhood trauma. As an adult, Nash began dating a woman and found himself struggling with feelings of confusion. His nervous system had entered a freeze response after two years of them being together.

As we explored his freeze response, Nash realized that his girlfriend treated him in the same manner that his father did, igniting past trauma. When he thought about leaving the relationship, he felt intense anxiety and then stopped taking action. Through mindfulness, Nash was able to realize that although he loved his father and his girlfriend as people, they were not the types of relationships he wanted to have in his life. Nash worked with his freeze response and was eventually able to get his own apartment and end the relationship with his girlfriend.

As children, our hearts are so wide open and curious that love pours out without any judgment. This feeling of unbounded open-heartedness arises when we are part of something bigger than ourselves. You may have had this open-hearted feeling at the sight of majestic mountains with clouds rolling over them or while gazing across the expanse of the ocean. These expansive, heart-centered feelings may arise looking at the spectacular rings of Saturn or the heart-shape in Pluto, or when you feel the tenderness and intimacy of gazing into the eyes of a baby for the first time. There is a quality of awe and wonder in this feeling of unbounded heart.

Loving-kindness similarly creates a sense of oneness. It's an awareness that you are beyond your physical body or your personal life. You are one with everything and everyone around you. It's as if you have melted into this world and you are in an altered state without taking plant medicine. Without your volition, your heart just pours out love to everyone and everything. Isn't it amazing to consider that as a child you were naturally created to feel this way? This state of being high on love is your true nature.

American Buddhist teacher Jack Kornfield calls this state of being *loving awareness*. It's the almost euphoric feeling where well-wishes pour out of your heart toward everyone and everything. You have no wish of harm—even to the fly that is buzzing around your head, the sand fleas biting at your feet at the beach, the boss who is threatening you with a harsh review, or soldiers who are at war with each other. This does not mean it is easy to live with your feet in two boats. One is the open, unbounded heart where the light of love is pouring in all directions while the other requires you to set boundaries with people or things that may harm you. These boundaries are essential for creating a sense of safety where your tender and vulnerable heart can remain open.

Cultivating loving-kindness means understanding when your heart is open and when your heart feels closed. Do you remember what it was like to be a child? Was your heart full of curiosity for this world around you as you explored it with wonder and awe? Do you remember the first time you ever saw a leaf swirling in the wind? Perhaps you chased after it, or maybe you ran away with fear, not knowing what it was. You may have experienced a sense of magic and wonder the first time water escaped from your small, closed fist as you tried to hold it. You may have laughed from the overwhelming sensation of feeling ice on your tongue for the first time. Take a moment and see if you can recall any of these "firsts" or other early memories where you were filled with that sense of awe and wonder. Do your best to recall a time when you lived with a trusting, unquestioning, open heart.

You can be in the state of having an open heart, or you can have a closed heart. What thoughts and emotions can you think of that lead to a closed heart? When you don't feel safe, your heart closes. If there is a threat—whether it is a real threat, a potential threat such as your beloved leaving you or someone harming you, or an imagined threat—your heart will naturally close. Safety is an essential ingredient to an open heart. That's why it's essential for us to receive safe and secure love and bonding from our parents as babies. So many of our painful traumas from our past, both remembered and unremembered, are layered and impact the way we show up in our present life. Like ghosts from the past, our woundings in love are often not only about the current relationship we're in.

Buddhism talks about the various ways our heart closes and names that feeling *hatred*. It is called the far enemy, or the opposite of loving-kindness. When I heard about this strong emotion, I shied away from it because I hadn't felt it in my life. I later realized that hatred has a purpose, to close my heart, and it comes disguised as different emotions like jealousy, hostility, dislike, resentment, and ill will. I honestly couldn't say that I had never felt these feelings, especially after working in capitalistic corporations where competition thrived.

In addition, Buddhism uses a fine-toothed comb to bring our awareness to feelings that appear to be similar to loving-kindness but also close off our heart. This is the near enemy of loving-kindness, and it is attachment. For example, in any relationship, we may assume that we are feeling loving-kindness, but underneath it we are holding on to something. There is a sense of trade. We think, *My beloved will marry me if I love them*, or, *My parents would have loved me if I got good grades or behaved well in their social circle.*

Attachment toward someone is not the same as feeling loving-kindness toward them because attachment comes with conditions, exclusivity, or the desire to receive some benefit. Attachment often has an element of control to it, whereas loving-kindness is a pure love for all beings, regardless of the outcome. Be aware of the unfolding of your loving heart that may occur as you go through your trauma healing. You may face the near and far enemies along your journey, but your authentic self has a blooming lotus heart.

Using Loving-Kindness to Work with Trauma

I shared the story of my meditation mentor, Premvarni, in the previous section to illustrate that even if we devote our lives to becoming the embodiment of love, there are still real, earthly challenges that make it a difficult state to maintain at all times. I encourage you to be gentle with yourself and give yourself permission to slide out of the feelings of loving-kindness as you go through your trauma healing. Loving-kindness is not meant to feel like a rule for living, but rather an inspiring goal as you are continuously moving toward your authentic self.

There are many factors that influence an individual's journey to open their heart to states of loving-kindness. One of those factors is their Buddhist personality type. In the most general of terms, the Peacemaker type will have the easiest time working toward loving-kindness as their motivation to move toward pleasant or unpleasant flavors of experience is not strong. They are not easily caught up in strong emotions of anger, jealousy, or hatred, nor are they caught up in attachment to people and material accomplishments. Their hearts are relatively free. With some purification, they can access love, kindness, benevolence, generosity, and compassion.

If the Optimists are able to rein in their attachment to beautiful people and things, they may more easily be able to hold this space of loving-kindness not only for others but for themselves as well. They have the ability to focus on the positive aspects of their being and tend to be less self-critical.

Conversely, the Strategist type may struggle the most with loving-kindness, particularly as it relates to feelings of self-love. Remember that the Strategist has the capacity to stay present with an unpleasant flavor of experiences so that they can identify potential harm and create optimal solutions. As protectors, their drive to create safety for others and their environment may create a sense of hypervigilance. In addition, their perfectionist personality doesn't let them rest and can result in self-criticism, the opposite of loving-kindness, which may close their heart. Strategist types should be extra gentle with themselves when it comes to opening their tender heart with the exercises in this chapter.

Those who engage in heart-opening loving-kindness meditation practices may tend to gloss over the need for boundaries. It may appear seemingly contradictory advice to open your vast, unbounded heart and also build up boundary walls. But boundaries are not inconsistent with loving-kindness. In fact, they are essential for your vulnerable and tender heart to bloom.

My client Luna was a Strategist who worked hard to maintain harmony in her home. While she was generally very loving, nurturing, and positive with her friends and coworkers, she realized that she was starting to feel depressed and irritated at home. She deeply loved her husband and had supported him through the recent loss of a family member. His challenges were compounded by difficulties at his job, leaving him feeling sad, confused, and moody. In our explorations during sessions, we soon realized that Luna was resonating with her husband's moods and feeling his feelings. When she blew up at her husband, it was interesting that her husband asked her, "Why are you being so moody?" These were the exact words she had wanted to say to him. She realized that their feelings had become enmeshed.

At the same time, Luna was also taking care of her elderly father. He had experienced a bad fall and was calling her every evening detailing his mobility challenges. Luna deeply loved her father, but the daily calls left her feeling helpless because she lived far away and couldn't provide direct support. The stress disrupted her sleep at night.

In her sessions with me, we spoke about her boundaries with the people in her life. Luna realized that she might feel better by setting the simple but loving request that her father call her during her lunch hour rather than at night when she was winding down. This boundary allowed her to support her father while also tending to her own needs. Her father was happy to accommodate the request. To address her own feelings of inadequacy for not being a "good daughter" and supporting him more, she began to ask more specific questions about what he actually needed. She found that he had clear ideas about what his care should look like and though she didn't agree with him, she decided to advocate for him with his medical team.

Luna realized that her feelings about love and how to express love were deeply rooted in her childhood experiences. Her white father was stoic and did not openly express his emotions. Conversely, her Filipino mother had large and loud emotional expressions, pulling everyone into her emotional state.

This was an important insight for Luna as she realized that she was blowing up at her husband in the same way that her mother used to blow up at her and her father. Luna realized that this reaction was not an expression of her authentic love and was instead a reflection of her taking on other people's emotions. To move past her childhood conditioning, Luna realized that she wanted to express an open-hearted feeling of loving-kindness toward everyone in her life, including herself.

While it takes constant work, Luna has now developed a greater awareness of her own emotions and is more attuned to the times when she begins picking up the emotions of others. She also continually works on setting boundaries to ensure safety for her own heart to blossom in loving-kindness to the people around her and to bathe in her own self-love.

———

When working with trauma or past conditioning, it's essential to nurture ourselves with loving-kindness. Trauma gives us an opportunity to turn the gentle warmth of unconditional love toward our wounded parts. If we did not receive proper guidance or were harmed as a child, then it is natural to not know how to love ourselves and love others at the same time. With the same tender care as a mother would offer her precious child, we can tend to those lost and broken aspects of ourselves. Though we may not have received the guidance to live a healthy life, now as an adult we have an inkling of what is wholesome. We feel it in ourselves.

Our love guides us toward this wholeness. It is a journey and not a destination. When trauma is present, we offer tenderness to our injuries as often as they arise. With Luna, she did not learn healthy boundaries as a child. As an adult she learned to take small steps by asking her husband what was happening with him, while balancing herself by not picking up his emotions in resonance. With her father, she learned the same lesson of asking about his needs without collapsing under his unspoken wants and desires.

Setting boundaries isn't easy as you may fear that you will lose your loved ones. You may have been enmeshed with your mother as a baby because you did not know what your needs were. As an adult, you may have a hard time identifying your needs. When I started working with clients in 2003, I would be wiped out for hours after giving one session. I had no energy and the emotions of my client would cycle through me. I realized that I had poor boundaries and needed to change the way I worked to create a healthier physical, emotional, and energetic space for myself. Today, I just need a few minutes to get water or tea between clients to recenter myself and be fully present for the next session.

Growing this inner knowing of yourself takes time and loving-patience. You can start your journey of setting boundaries with the Mindfulness Tool below on Standing your Ground. If you are not used to setting good boundaries as part of your self-care, then you'll be surprised to find that it is a long and slow journey, but incredibly worthwhile. Though my journey took years of practice to reach this point, you may be able to achieve it faster by practicing some of these suggestions.

✿ Mindfulness Tool: Standing Your Ground

To create healthier boundaries in your life, it is essential for you to know your own physical, mental, emotional, and energetic space. You may wish to journal your thoughts for the first few prompts and revisit this mindfulness practice regularly.

1. **Recognize:** The first step to identifying where you may need a boundary in your life is to recognize where you feel the pinch of being overextended. This may be a mental, physical, or emotional discomfort. Identify if you have had any recent experiences that may indicate a boundary breach, such as your boss making an unrealistic demand, your elderly parent requesting more of your time than you had available, or a fitness class where you pushed yourself beyond a comfortable physical limit to not disappoint the teacher.

2. **Listen:** When you feel these moments of overextension, take a moment to pause and listen to what is happening in your body and mind. Notice your thought patterns and the emotions you're feeling. Listening to and becoming familiar with these sensations will help to alert you more easily in the future when a boundary has been violated. Rather than confront the other person immediately in these situations, consider journaling or speaking to a trusted friend or therapist who will listen fully.

3. **Check in with your nervous system:** What are the emotions or sensations that you identified as you listened to yourself or that your friend or therapist helped you identify as they listened to you deeply? It is likely that if you noticed anger, your body could be in a fight response. If you felt fear, you may be in a flight

response. If you found it challenging to identify your emotions, found your thoughts to be incoherent, or experienced several confusing emotions, you could be in a freeze response.

4. **Express:** Bring in some movement and see if that helps you alleviate these trauma responses. Initially you may move quickly, but then I suggest you slow down to activate your parasympathetic nervous system. Along with the physical expressions, bring in some vocal expressions like singing, humming, or chanting. These are exercises you are doing by yourself. Once you have fully expressed your emotions and your mind is clear, then you can find appropriate, nonconfrontational words to express yourself to the person who is breaching your boundary, just like Luna did with her husband and her father.

5. **Build strength:** If you were to set up a physical boundary, like a wall, to protect yourself, you would engage the muscles of your shoulders, biceps, and triceps. Performing exercises that activate these muscles signal to your body and mind that you are establishing protective barriers. You may try movements like pushing against a wall while practicing "no" statements that you could use with others to establish a boundary. It may be things like, "No, I am unable to help with that today," or, "No, I am not interested in that opportunity." The combination of physical movement with voice activation may empower you with future boundary setting.

✿ Mindfulness Tool: Cultivating an Open Heart

This exercise is one that I have made a part of my daily practice. It allows my heart to abide in its natural state of being vulnerable, open, and unbounded. Find a comfortable, quiet space to do this work.

1. The traditional loving-kindness mantra is: "May you be safe, may you be healthy, may you be happy, may you be at ease." I suggest that you start by creating your own loving-kindness phrases in the language you grew up with, especially if you are bilingual. Using your native language taps the awe and wonder residing in the heart of your inner child. You may want to imagine two loving people standing beside you, placing their hands on your shoulders. This allows your supported heart to release past pain and welcome aliveness, spontaneity, and vulnerability.

2. You may imagine your beloved is sitting before you. You know what they truly want in their life: love, an inner sense of safety, a strong body, health, happiness, a calm mind, an unbound heart, joy, laughter, mischief, play, and so on. Using your own words, wish them all these qualities. Sense how your heart feels. Do you feel it blossom with love and joy? This is just the beginning of the gift of loving-kindness practice.

3. Next, imagine sitting before your friends and offering them loving-kindness. Then move to your pets, your friends, your family, your community, and even strangers with whom you've had casual interactions. After you offer each person loving-kindness, check in with your heart to see how you feel.

4. Next, offer loving-kindness to someone you feel a little irritated with. As you do your practice regularly, and you have people in your life who fit the description, then you can move up the scale of irritation to people who make you angry or rageful. The practice of loving-kindness with these people may close your heart, so bring back some images of the people whose presence in your life makes your heart smile and makes you happy.

5. Now expand to include your communities of various kinds, such as your neighbors, meditation community, young parents community, addicts community, environmentally friendly

community, or social media community. You may have too many communities to pick from! Choose one, and then expand your heart to include all the people in this country and all over the world.

6. Lastly, send loving-kindness to the most important beings with whom you share this planet: the grasses, plants, trees, insects, birds, animals, fishes. Wish these beings all the goodness they desire and much more! May we live in harmony with them! If you feel so drawn, you can send your love vibration to the stars and planets in our galaxy and beyond.

How does your heart feel? Does it expand so much that your chest isn't large enough to hold it? Is the radiation of love emanating from your entire being? Is benevolence and compassion flowing from you? That is the true essence of you: a kind and loving heart that is large enough to hold this entire world and still have space within it. Meet your own unbound heart!

The Journey of Loving-Kindness

When you practice loving-kindness, you'll be surprised to find that it is an antidote to both selfishness and anger. You'll find that you are open-hearted and generous and have more pleasure in giving and sharing than keeping things to yourself. In practicing loving-kindness, you are not only extending love to yourself but also to everyone and everything around you. There is a certain sense of oneness with everyone and everything around you.

I have noticed in my own work with loving-kindness that sometimes the things that irritated me the most about others have softened over time and may even be amusing. The open-hearted space within me is vast enough to hold the irritating person, but this space is not ready to close down anymore. If I feel an interaction with someone is closing my heart, I become curious about the aspects the other person is mirroring. I know that those aspects probably exist within me, but there is a part of me that does not wish to claim them as my own.

In a purification process, loving-kindness allows me to claim my grief, anger, fear, negativity, and humanity without acting it out. Once I have claimed my own inner turmoil, the natural tenderness and benevolence within my own heart can flow more easily toward myself and others. It's fascinating to get to explore the rhythm of my heart like a night-blooming jasmine that blooms at night and releases its strong, sweet fragrance and closes during the day. Practicing loving-kindness is a moment-to-moment lifelong journey, but one that is absolutely enjoyable to take.

Compassion

You yourself, as much as anybody in the entire universe, deserve your love and affection.

—Buddha

When your heart opens with loving-kindness, it naturally quivers at the sight of someone else's pain and you have a strong desire to do something and relieve their pain. This deep-seated urge is the Buddhist Sublime State of compassion. Our open heart fills with loving-kindness and becomes naturally interconnected with all beings, desiring safety, security, and harmony for all. But some meaning gets lost when the Sanskrit and Pali word *karuna* is translated to "compassion" in English. Beyond just compassion, it's a state of being that encompasses empathy, understanding, and the desire to alleviate suffering and pain. It is the urge to take some action that arises from the state of open-heartedness.

When we feel compassion, it brings us into connection with ourselves and others. With the interconnected heart of loving-kindness, we are able to tap into the truth that whatever we're going through, thousands or even millions of people around the world are facing the same situation. We let loose our loneliness and isolation and begin to feel connected to ourselves and others. This happened with my client, Selena.

Selena was a nonbinary, transgender person who was assigned female at birth and chose to present in that gender identity at work. They held a high-powered job in the business world that would not have welcomed their inner identity. They had been hiding themself since childhood; however, the toll of being so different internally and externally was beginning to seriously affect their mental and physical health. This included causing recurring nightmares several times a week. Selena felt a strong sense of shame that caused them to hide, leaving them feeling disconnected from the people they loved.

When I started working with Selena, we role played to help them imagine what they would do or say to themself if they were being honest and compassionate toward themself. They felt the deep colonization of their body, and over time realized they could no longer maintain this outer disconnect from their true nature. Selena found the courage to share their true identity with their husband.

Much to Selena's surprise, their husband already suspected they were trans and was very accepting. Selena moved out of the household but stayed close friends and confidants with their ex-husband. Slowly and with gentle encouragement, Selena came out to the friends and family members whom they felt sure would be accepting. With each acceptance and affirmation of their identity, their confidence rose. They became more comfortable with their unique skin, body, and bones. Their nightmares began to subside.

Selena became curious about their self-discovery and traveled several hours to the San Francisco Bay area to connect with the large and open transgender community there. As Selena mourned the years lost in hiding their identity, they deepened into self-compassion. Soon, other trans people in their community sought them out, and they were able to guide these young people on their own journeys to being their authentic selves.

At one point, Selena had a car accident and broke several bones in their body. While they were recovering, their trans friends supported them with household chores. Selena continued to be a confidant, and listening to their stories, Selena's heart broke wide open. Despite their physical pain and immobility, Selena continued to mentor the younger members of the group. This was an important part of their dedication to self-compassion. They continued their inner healing work as well as guiding others.

———

Feeling into your truth can bring a sense of connection, not only to yourself and your lived experience, but to so many others in your human family around the world. For example, if you have lost your job, then the helplessness, frustration, desperation, and shame you feel is shared by thousands of others who have also lost their jobs and seek new employment. If in the midst of this sorrow, you can tune into this feeling of connectedness with others, then it can bring you out of loneliness, isolation, and feelings of "why me." Self-compassion has the capacity to not only soothe your heart and mind, but to be a healing balm to your soul.

As we grow in our awareness and our heart continues to open, we may feel compassion toward others suffering even when it's not tied to our own. This sense of connection activates the social engagement nervous system and gives us more access to our thinking brain. In this safe state of our nervous system, our mind opens to creative solutions and unlimited possibilities. It is an empowering place to be.

The opposite of compassion, or its far enemy, is cruelty. Sometimes we see images of cruelty from wars being fought on our planet and our heart cannot bear the suffering of others. We are horrified when we see humans do terrible things to each other. We may hide by ignoring the news altogether or we collapse, shut down, or cry uncontrollably, unable to get up from the sofa.

When you see someone else's life being threatened, your gut-based dorsal vagal nervous system is turned on and your body interprets it as if your own life is in danger. This has the potential to send you into a freeze or dissociated state. If you have found that you experience this extreme empathetic response to acts of cruelty, then it is likely that you're already a very compassionate person. You may feel others' experiences deeply in your body, and your open heart may desire to help them. In situations of conflict or cruelty that occur far away, your compassion may elicit feelings of helplessness.

To maintain your sense of compassion and not overextend your heart, you may wish to slowly bring more balance to your life through a regular compassion practice. Incorporating gentle movement and setting a boundary on the news that your nervous system can handle will bring you out of the freeze response. The challenge of compassion is that sometimes we prioritize compassion for others and lose sight of the compassion we owe ourselves. One such example of this comes from my own practice and my client Basil.

Basil is a British journalist who had settled in Colombia and covered news for newspapers and magazines back home. His vast compassionate heart took him to areas of the continent that were considered unsafe for nonlocal journalists. He contributed to exposing how marginalized populations had been uprooted by government atrocities, acts that had previously been unknown to the rest of the world.

Basil was excited to finally take three months off and explore various parts of Brazil. This novel adventure required Basil to move to a new Airbnb every few days or weeks. What he did not anticipate was that each move to a new, unfamiliar setting would trigger feelings of anxiety. The initial feelings of excitement soon turned to feelings of destabilization. He began to experience sleepless nights from staying in other people's homes. Unfortunately, even once he returned home, his sleepless nights persisted. His nervous system was in a constant state of high alert.

Basil found himself in a challenging conundrum. While his overactive nervous system kept him awake, his inner critic scared him into believing he would become addicted to sleeping pills if he took one. Due to his inner critic, he would experience another sleepless night, further taxing his already exhausted mind and body. This perpetuated an even louder and more critical inner voice.

I worked with Basil to practice mindfulness techniques that would help shift his nervous system state. By the end of our sessions, he would often find himself yawning and would sleep deeply that night. The empathetic and nonjudgmental support during our sessions allowed his nervous system to relax for a short time before the ruminating cycle of sleeplessness and self-criticism would ensue.

I gently encouraged Basil to seek additional support from a medical doctor and psychiatrist. Both assured Basil that taking occasional sleeping pills would not turn him into an addict and would be a helpful tool in getting much-needed sleep to calm and reset his nervous system.

Though Basil was deeply compassionate toward the people of Colombia whose plight he reported on, he lacked self-compassion and this prevented him from basic self-care. When he reached the edge of his mental and physical capacity, he was eventually able to be compassionate and allow himself to try the sleep medication. Getting better sleep, combined with mindfulness techniques and gentle encouragement from his support team, made him feel safe and turned on his social engagement nervous system so he could maintain a calm, safe, and relaxed state of mind.

There can be multiple hidden reasons for lack of self-compassion, including an inner critic that feels that you are undeserving of rest or self-care or drives you to accomplish tasks with its razor-sharp censorship. Your harsh inner critic can drive you harder when you are sick or emotionally vulnerable. This pummeling can leave you feeling ungrounded and doubting your own decisions, meaning you are unable to choose what is beneficial for yourself. In this confusion, it is difficult to determine which actions are part of self-care because the inner critic has labeled them as being weak or self-indulgent.

A strong inner critic is a barrier to self-compassion and compassion toward others. If you find yourself stuck in the grip of the inner critic, then I suggest practicing the compassion exercises at the end of this chapter. Self-love and self-compassion may not come to you instantaneously, but every small effort in that direction has rewards of cultivating inner peace and harmony over time.

One final challenge with compassion is its near enemy: pity, the emotion that can be easily mistaken for compassion. When we feel bad for someone and are compassionate toward that person, it's a good time to inquire whether our actions are based on our heart's response or if we are intellectualizing a situation. In both situations, your action may be kind to the other person, but your motivation can vary. Pity is an emotion laced with feelings of superiority, disdain, or slight contempt for the person. Our hearts are not engaged when we feel pity.

An open-hearted desire to do something to alleviate the suffering of others is truly the quiver of a compassionate heart. For example, if we see an unhoused person who seems to be talking to an invisible being, the response of pity might be to see their mental state and walk away quickly while complaining about the city not housing people with mental health issues. A person who experiences pity for another is unlikely to feel a strong sense of empathy and may even throw a few coins at the unhoused person to appease their own conscience.

Because pity moves you out of a state of oneness with those around you, it is a near enemy to living and embodying the Sublime State of compassion. It robs you of the knowing that we are all made of the same building blocks: earth, water, fire, air, and space. The only difference between your life and that of the unhoused person is that they experienced a slight change to the algorithm so that they became unhoused and you didn't. A job loss followed by a multitude of other difficulties can make you lose the safety and security of your home. The same consciousness inhabits both you and the unhoused person. When you touch into this deeper reality, then your heart opens and quivers at the sad state of the unhoused person—this is compassion arising. You deeply feel that helping this person is the same as helping yourself.

Compassion in action arises when you realize that you are made of the same cloth as the other person and their pain and suffering is like a thread that has come loose. Your natural urge is to weave the thread back into the cloth and to harmonize this cloth we call humanity. This compassionate heart changes the way you operate in the world. You may take the same action of giving them a few dollars, but your action arises from a different underlying heart space.

When you witness senseless death and destruction in your community or on TV, instead of going into despondency or despair or even anger and rage, you can turn toward your compassionate heart and see what you can do to alleviate the suffering. Is it time to join a protest march, post on social media, or contribute to a GoFundMe campaign to feed the hungry and clothe the children impacted by the war? Is your best course of action to sit in a compassion meditation and offer love and blessings as your heart breaks for humanity?

There are times when we desire to be compassionate toward others but feel too exhausted. This is known as *compassion fatigue*, which is also called secondary traumatic stress or vicarious trauma. It is common in healthcare professional, caregivers of all kinds, social workers, and other individuals who are exposed to high levels of human suffering on a regular basis. Compassion fatigue can manifest as emotional detachment, numbness, insomnia, headaches, reduced empathy and compassion, difficulty concentrating, increased anxiety and depression, burnout, or cynicism. It can be managed through a combination of self-care practices, boundary setting, and support seeking. Prioritizing personal well-being through activities like exercise, healthy eating, and quality sleep, while also incorporating mindfulness and relaxation techniques, is crucial. Additionally, establishing clear boundaries between work and personal life, seeking support from colleagues or support groups, and actively engaging in activities that bring joy can help combat the negative effects of compassion fatigue.

Most of us who have been through traumatic events know what it feels like to not be held in the compassionate embrace of an empathetic other. As you start your own healing journey to reignite your power, you first feel the touch of your own suffering and open to self-love. You reading this chapter is an expression of that self-love. You then start to experience self-compassion, and that motivates you to take on practices of self-care. From self-compassion, you enlarge your circle of care, as you start feeling compassion toward people around you. Soon your compassionate heart includes the people in your greater community, your country, and across the world. It takes a large heart to open to the plight of the people suffering in countries impacted by war, famine, climate crisis, or natural disaster. Maybe your compassionate heart will be inspired to support other people in creative ways and instill a little more harmony in their lives.

Using Compassion to Work with Trauma

Compassion is not a state that we turn on and off like an electrical switch. As we cultivate our compassionate heart, it affects the way we view the world and our interactions with others. Our trauma, however, may present challenges in tapping into our compassion as our amygdala is on the lookout for potential threats based on our past experiences. We may not have access to self-compassion immediately in the midst of a difficult situation when the amygdala goes into survival mode.

I encourage you to cultivate compassion practices ahead of time so that you have access to them when you do face difficult life challenges, just as my client Melody did.

———————

Melody found working with compassion to be an important part of her own healing journey. Melody had health issues and had begun experiencing seizures. She was subjected to a barrage of medical tests of her brain to determine the root cause of the seizures, including being kept awake for three straight days and nights in a lab.

While this would have been an incredibly stressful experience for anyone, Melody decided to deepen her mindfulness practice by deepening her connection with Quan Yin, the Chinese Buddhist goddess of compassion who listens to the painful cries of everyone. During her three days of sleeplessness in the brain lab, she remained free from seizures even though the conditions were meant to induce seizures so that she could be studied and appropriately treated for them.

Melody attributed this to hearing Quan Yin chanting beside her. This chant held her heart with compassion and created a sense of safety and joy. In the presence of the archetypal mother of compassion, she went into a timeless space and though fatigued, she did not feel stress. Melody later carried the energy of Quan Yin's compassion with her as she went into brain surgery, where doctors removed a tumor that was causing her seizures.

Before all this, Melody had experienced a difficult childhood as a Native American whose family faced a lot of hardships. In their attempt to make ends meet, her loving parents held multiple jobs and did not spend sufficient time with the children, who grew up on their own. Self-compassion did not initially come easily to Melody, who considered it a weakness. Her attitude was more "get on with it." Melody was a pragmatic Strategist type who cut herself off from many of her feelings in order to survive through challenging times.

When it came to her difficult health challenge, her "get on with it" attitude was not helping her. This was when Melody realized she could no longer suppress her pain or ignore her needs. She began to reach out to Quan Yin. While Melody could not cry for herself at first, she felt the mother of compassion holding her and supporting her and shedding tears for her. It was an important step in her understanding that she was worthy of loving-kindness and compassion.

Self-love is a prerequisite to self-compassion. Regardless of your primary Buddhist personality type, we all could use more self-love and self-compassion. However, if you're a Strategist type, you may find that your inner critic adds an additional layer to your struggles with self-love. Don't let this be discouraging to you, though. Use this awareness to create safety and self-care, just as you would for your loved ones, friends, and family. This awareness and permission to support yourself with self-compassion will lead you down the unique path of healing and empowerment that you deserve.

✿ Mindfulness Tool: Practicing Self-Compassion

Imagine if each word you said to yourself was a prayer or wish for you. Would you speak to yourself with more loving-kindness and compassion? Compassion, especially self-compassion, doesn't come easily to most of us. If you feel you could use some self-compassion, then try this practice.

1. **Situation:** Begin by imagining yourself facing a difficult situation. It may be one you're presently experiencing or one from the past.

2. **Emotion:** Identify your predominant feeling in this experience. Do you feel broken? Alone? Lonely? Empty?

3. **Your younger self:** If this is a familiar and past experience, check in to see how old you are. Determine who is feeling these feelings. Is it you or are you picking up the emotions of someone around you? Whatever the case, see yourself at that age.

4. **Support:** Now place a hand on your heart and the other on your belly. Breathe into these areas until you feel your body begin to relax. As your body calms down, notice if your thoughts and emotions are settling as well. How have they changed?

5. **Expand:** Now imagine people in India, China, South Africa, Finland, Brazil, or other countries where others may have the same loss, grief, or difficulty. Sense how you are not alone in this pain and suffering. Notice if this connection alleviates the feelings of loneliness and isolation. Does it give you the feeling of being back in the fold of the human family who have experienced similar suffering?

6. **Love:** You know better than anyone else what you need to feel loved and comforted. Imagine either your beloved, your therapist, your teacher, or your adult self offering this love and comfort to you or to your inner child.

7. **Compassion:** See what is needed to soothe your complaint or injured heart. The traditional Buddhist phrase for self-compassion is, "May I be free from suffering." If these words don't resonate with you then you might say, "It's okay. I'll be okay. I'm doing the best I can." I encourage you to create your own phrases that express self-compassion by wishing peace, safety, patience, and kindness toward yourself.

If you are unable to offer words of comfort to yourself, then try to imagine what someone who dearly loves you would say to you. What words could they say that would soothe you? Imagine you are offering these compassionate words to some of the eight billion people on our planet who may be going through the same heartbreak or suffering as yours. See if you can tap into the oneness with humanity so that you don't feel alone during this difficult time.

If this self-compassion practice soothed your heart, then you can return to it regularly to continue opening your heart to self-compassion. If English is your second language, then writing out a few phrases in your primary language will help reach your inner child.

☸ Mindfulness Tool: Tapping Exercise for Compassion

The Emotional Freedom Technique (EFT) is a trauma healing technique that combines acupressure with cognitive behavioral therapy (CBT) to release emotional and physical pain. Through tapping on specific acupressure points on the body while focusing on current negative emotions or situations, you release those patterns and can replace them with new belief patterns. Due to the specific pressure points, tapping also activates the parasympathetic nervous system. In the following EFT script, you start out by noticing and naming what is present for you and then transition to finding new possibilities for your mind and heart.

Start out by sensing your body and see where you feel grounded and connected. It may be in your chest or your knees or the bottoms of your feet. If none of the places in your body stand out, then feel into your breath and the movement of your chest and belly. Take a few breaths in the part of your body that feels grounded and deeply connected to the great Mother Earth.

Notice how safe or unsafe you feel at this moment. Even if right now there is no elephant charging toward you or someone coming to harm you, you may feel unsafe and want to run for the hills. If you had to rate your sense of safety from 0 to 10, with 0 being completely unsafe, where would you rank your current feeling?

Let's begin tapping. Tap gently and keep a moderate rhythm. If you are relaxed and go through this practice slowly, your parasympathetic nervous system's relaxation response will turn on more easily.

Using the fingertips of one hand, begin tapping on the side of your other hand. You can switch hands after a minute or so if you'd like to feel the sensation in both hands. While tapping, say these statements out loud:

Side of hand	Even though I feel unsafe in my body and my heart is racing and hands are shaking, I accept myself in this moment, and I'm doing the best I can to be present with myself.
	Even though this lack of safety is familiar and feelings of safety are unfamiliar and unreal to me, I have heard about safety, so I know it is possible. I am willing to explore the idea of safety. I am willing to trust that I can be safe.

Continue tapping by moving to different parts of the face and body, saying the phrase associated with each area aloud. If you slowly say the phrase while tapping the same point, you may find that you are tapping three to five times on the same spot, which is usually sufficient to shift your nervous system.

Eyebrows (where your nose meets your eyebrows)	I just don't feel safe;
Sides of eyes (simultaneously on both of your temples located on the sides of the head, specifically between the forehead and the ear and above the cheekbone)	With my past history,
Under eyes (on the bone of both eye sockets below your eyes)	safety hasn't been possible.
Under nose (between nose and lips)	I've been through a lot in my life,

Under mouth (below your lips but above your chin)	and I just don't know how to feel safe.
Collarbone (below your collarbone on both sides)	Safety hasn't been part of my life.
Under arms (cross your arms across your chest and tap both sides of your rib cage)	I would rather distract myself.
Top of head (use several fingers)	I would rather hide or run away.

Repeat the same tapping sequence with new phrases:

Eyebrows	It's not safe to feel my body sensations.
Side of eyes	I feel so much pain.
Under eyes	I feel so much discomfort.
Under nose	My body just wants to run and hide.
Under mouth	My body feels terrified.
Collarbone	My body does not feel safe.
Under arms	I do not feel safe.
Top of head	This lack of safety feels so familiar to me.

Eyebrows	It's not safe to feel my emotions.
Side of eyes	I don't know what I may say or do.
Under eyes	I feel out of control.
Under nose	I feel so broken.
Under mouth	I have been through so much.
Collarbone	I can't change my past.

Under arms	What's the point in trying to heal?
Top of head	Nothing will change. I feel so hopeless.

Eyebrows	All I want to do is give up.
Side of eyes	All I did was survive.
Under eyes	Somehow, I kept my body and soul together.
Under nose	But surviving got me this far.
Under mouth	And I am still here today.
Collarbone	What if I try this healing journey?
Under arms	What if I discover that I am not broken?
Top of head	I did all I could to survive.

Eyebrows	I came out of a very difficult past.
Side of eyes	What if I am gentle with myself,
Under eyes	and give myself credit for my struggle?
Under nose	What if I am really resilient?
Under mouth	Oh, that would make me cry.
Collarbone	I have come out of a lot of difficulty.
Under arms	That's all the more reason to be gentle with myself.
Top of head	I'm not used to being gentle with myself.

Eyebrows	I could try to soothe myself.
Side of eyes	There is nothing to fix.
Under eyes	There is nothing broken within me.
Under nose	I am Japanese kintsugi pottery.
Under mouth	Golden light is shining
Collarbone	through the cracks of pain in my body.
Under arms	I am whole.
Top of head	I am unique just as I am.

Eyebrows	I am safe in my own presence.
Side of eyes	I am grounded in my own love.
Under eyes	I tend to my needs.
Under nose	I am warmed by my own compassion.
Under mouth	I accept myself as I am.
Collarbone	There's no holding me back now!
Under arms	I am unlimited potential.
Top of head	I am healing in every moment.

After the tapping exercise, check in and see if your safety scale has shifted in a positive direction. If it has, then your self-love and self-compassion have triggered a healing cascade within you.

The Journey of Compassion

When we practice compassion, we have the ability to impact our nervous systems in a positive way. Compassion can help us move out of feelings of isolation, self-blame, self-criticism, and loneliness and into our social engagement nervous system. There, we feel safe in a greater connection to ourselves and others. Compassion connects us to the larger humanity and creates a feeling that we are engaged in the greater good. A compassionate heart supports us and supports others.

Compassion in action will lead to the release of oxytocin, the love hormone, which is released in our bodies when we feel safe, loved, and supported. Through this feeling of connectedness, our own pain is held, supported, and cared for. Then we are never alone!

Joy and Delight in Others' Happiness

All joy in this world comes from wanting others to be happy, and all suffering in this world comes from wanting only oneself to be happy.

—Shantideva

In our daily life we are constantly seeking joy and delight. This may be something as simple as scrolling through social media. In that time, hopefully you experienced some joy from reading or seeing something you found interesting, novel, or fascinating. Perhaps you check your phone multiple times today for text messages. In these moments you've experienced the Sublime State of joy (*mudita*) that comes from connecting with someone and knowing they're thinking about you.

These seemingly everyday, ordinary moments of joy were everywhere in the life of my friend, Merijane. She is a twenty-year metastatic cancer survivor, and I can say that I have never seen anyone enjoy life like she does. Merijane's eyes light up as she listens fully to someone with all of her being. She savors every bite of a meal and bathes in light every time the sun is out. Nothing is left out. Merijane lives by the words of American poet and prose writer Mary Oliver who said, "If you suddenly and unexpectedly feel joy, don't hesitate. Give in to it."

While we may soak up these brief moments of temporary joy, they are just that—ephemeral. Here and then gone. These moments of joy make us feel vibrant, but their fleeting nature has us quickly searching for the next post or message that might bring us a slight thrill of aliveness. All the while, we could have been living and moving toward ways to create continuous joy, awe, and wonder as a regular part of our lives. I am certainly not advising you to get off of social media or ignore those text messages, but I do encourage you to also seek ways to bring this satiating joy into your life in other ways.

The Dalai Lama has said that when we celebrate, delight, and feel joy in the successes and happiness of others, then the chances of our own happiness increasing are very high. Buddhism refers to this delight in the joy of others as *sympathetic joy*. While achieving a regular state of joy takes some effort, the act of feeling sympathetic joy is quite simple. It can even be done when you're feeling tired or lazy. Quite simply, you lie on your sofa and experience this joy bubbling within you by remembering the good things that have happened to others. You might remember a joyful moment with your friends or hearing the delightful squeal of a child at the park. You might recall the surprised smile you received when you handed the stranger the last loaf of bread in the grocery aisle or your dog bounding toward you when you entered the house. As you remember these things, you feel gladness in your heart.

Due to the simplicity and ease of this practice, I have a plaque on my fridge that reads, "Don't Postpone Joy!" It is a daily reminder to engage in daily laughter and joyful activities. When I come home at the end of my day, I can rest on my sofa and remember the good things that happened that day and multiply my happiness even more by practicing sympathetic joy. Joy can be easy to find, but we must be the ones to look for it.

My client Zach was born prematurely. For the first month of his life he was kept in an incubator, physically separated from receiving touch and connection with the world around him. As an adult, Zach continued to feel an intense need for love, though the real connection from a relationship always seemed to be out of reach and he struggled to find meaningful relationships.

Through our mindfulness work together, Zach realized that his feelings of desperation to connect with others had kept him from connecting with himself first. Rather than chasing external validation, Zach had to step away from dating and learn who he was and what brought him joy. This came through his artistic expression of composing songs and playing music, which gave him a sense of fullness and delight.

Eventually, Zach expanded this feeling of joy and connection by joining a band. He found great joy in sharing his musical instruments with the band members and brought them together to record an album. This joy in music spread to other areas of Zach's life. He felt inspired to grow his business in helping special needs children, which felt deeply satisfying to him. He found great joy in working with children and turning their lives around at such a young age! Our sessions together went from a focus on lack of relationships to his dreams and plans in creating a life of connection, love, and fullness, which the baby in the incubator was missing.

Zach was searching for his bliss in a relationship with his beloved. The challenge was that this source of bliss was ephemeral and dependent upon the actions of another person. When Zach was able to open to a stream of consistent joy within himself, he then found his own happiness in the delight of others. Instead of seeking his bliss externally in the next relationship, he stumbled on the joy of seeing his friends enjoy playing his musical instruments and the rapture of his audience captivated by his sound healing music. He said he began to hear the song of the grass, song of the trees, song of the ocean, and song of the universe, which further grew his feelings of joy. He wove these songs into the song of compassion when he played his blissful music. Zach's fears and insecurities had been replaced by a warmhearted fullness. He had tasted what the Dalai Lama refers to as the joy of interconnection.

☸ Mindfulness Tool: Recognizing Joy

I recognize and celebrate the joys in my own life and also delight in the wonderful people in my life. Grab your favorite journal, something to write with, and a cozy place to sit and try this joy tool.

1. **Daily Life Joy:** Start by thinking of the moments in your day or week that brought you joy. These are the moments when you felt yourself light up inside. Perhaps it was receiving an invitation to your neighbor's surprise birthday party or enjoying a leisurely meal with friends. Your joy may have come from personal or business success when you launched your new app or shared a funny video on social media that made others laugh. Joy can come from the simple, quiet moments like wading through the warm, salty water at the beach or hiking through the peaceful forest. Take a moment to think of and write down the many moments of sheer enjoyment, delight, and pleasure in your life. You may find that the more often you look for them and recount them, the more consciously you notice them and savor them longer.

2. **Sympathetic Joy:** Now make a list of your close friends and family members. For each person, make a list of their recent achievements, successes, or milestones. This list might include milestones in their relationships or academic success. Remember how each person felt when they shared these moments with you. Recall their delight and joy. See how you feel in your body when those memories arise. How do you feel when you remember those times? Write down any emotions and body sensations you feel or further memories that arise.

3. **Spiritual Joy in Daily Life:** In some traditions, the highest form of spiritual practice is in performing your daily life actions with joy and without attachment to the end results. While that's an

esoteric practice that is beyond the pages of this book, I wanted to introduce it here so that, if you are drawn to it, you can explore it further in your spiritual journey.

Using Joy to Work with Trauma

The practice of joy and delight may seem to be the easiest of the Four Sublime States in Buddhism. It often requires the least effort and yields the quickest return. At the same time, even joy may have its pitfalls. The near enemy of joy is comparison or jealousy. Sometimes, in an attempt to feel sympathetic joy and delight in others' happiness, we find ourselves feeling insincere or comparing ourselves with them. We may feel joy for them but then start desiring or coveting what they have.

In our modern world with social media, we often see the possessions and experiences of others who may live vastly different lives from us. That means this feeling of comparing with others and finding ourselves to be less than is very common. Teenagers live in a world of cyber competition with peers whom they will never meet. The distress caused by that jealousy is very difficult for their young hearts to handle, and feelings of inadequacy and self-loathing can arise. Our joyful open-heart closes, and it becomes more challenging to think rationally. We may find ourselves saying or doing things that we regret out of jealousy toward the other person. The true challenge of delighting in the joy of others is not to attach comparison to their experience and simply celebrate in their joy.

With the relative ease of joy, there is also a greater likelihood that our trauma can masquerade under the guise of joy. I see this most often appearing as one of the nervous system responses to trauma that is less talked about: the *fawn* response. Fawning, also known as appease response, is a complex trauma survival mechanism where an individual may try to please the perpetrator to avoid or de-escalate further conflict. While trauma often appears as fight, flight, or freeze, fawn is now being recognized as a trauma response in people who have experienced abuse themselves or of others. In fawn, a person may sacrifice their own needs in favor of their abuser's needs in an attempt to minimize future traumatic events. Sometimes, our trauma can masquerade under the guise of joy, especially as the fawn response, as in the case of Grace.

––––––––––––

Grace is an energetic and generous healer who enjoys helping others. One of her friends, Dave, suggested that they partner together in business. Grace felt this would be a beneficial relationship as Dave's business acumen could help take her fledgling business to the next level. This business relationship quickly began to extend into the personal realm, with Dave seeking Grace's support with helping him change his diet to address his physical illness. Grace happily complied, feeling that she was being of service to Dave. Dave's requests for Grace's time and energy increased. Grace would find herself listening to Dave talk about his life and needs while she played the patient (but frustrated) listener. With time, Grace realized that this business relationship had unexpectedly turned into her serving as Dave's unpaid therapist, cook, and healer.

Grace realized that she continued to opt in to Dave's requests, regardless of whether she really wanted to help or not, due to her fawn response. The joy of giving had trauma buried underneath it. Grace decided to end the business relationship with Dave and directly work with her fawn response by engaging in the powerful tools of spiritual self-inquiry and investigation. She uncovered her childhood patterns of caring for and appeasing her mother and worked to let them go. In the process, her relationships with her friends shifted. They were filled with love and compassion for Grace and were now able to offer her gifts and support. And Grace discovered the joy of receiving love and gifts from her friends instead of just offering it to them.

There is immense joy in giving, if, according to Gary Chapman, one of your love languages is acts of service where you anticipate which tasks you can perform so as to lighten the load of your beloved. If you are paired with a person who feels loved when they receive gifts, as with Grace and Dave, then the relationship can be very satisfying. For people who are experiencing a fawn trauma response, acts of service that may initially feel joyful can transform into excessively wanting to please. In Grace's story, Dave received more than he offered to Grace. This left her feeling overextended and fatigued rather than joyful. Grace came to realize that her fawn response would often show up in her body as an excruciating and hollow feeling in her belly. She learned that rather than acting out her fawn response, she could stay with the sensation in her belly. She was able to slowly fill this hollow space by slowing down the pace of her activities. She also became more vulnerable with her friends and shared that she did not feel good enough to let people do things for her. Grace's friends were patient and loving. They did not give up on her and slowly she was able to begin receiving acts of service from them. The hollow feeling began to dissipate.

In the process of her healing, Grace had tapped into the joy of giving *and* receiving, which arises from interconnection with each other and our communities. In the olden times, we were dependent on our neighbors for our own survival. Our lives were based in our community and not individualistic. Conversely, most modern societies have experienced a disconnect of community and even family. There is a push to develop independence without valuing the interdependence that has always been such a necessary part of our survival.

There is so much joy to be found in large gatherings and celebrations filled with music and food, as is still more commonplace in Asian and Latin cultures. Even people who were enslaved throughout history found strength through honoring their own pain and suffering through songs shared by the community. In the most horrible of times, joy has been created by fostering community and a sense of belonging and solidarity.

When we practice sympathetic joy, we drop into this interconnection with our loved ones and with all humanity. It is a new way to be alive on our planet and be connected to everyone, acknowledging our interdependence with each other. This is truly our essence and our reality. We are not individuals but part of a bigger picture on this planet. Individualism is a myth that doesn't hold true for us, nor for the countries we live in. The importance of our dependence on each other seems more glaring now than ever before because as a planet, we are one living organism that is part of a greater cosmos. When we truly touch into this reality, there is no space for loneliness, isolation, jealousy, or envy because our lived reality is "we" rather than "I." With joy for the joy of others, we automatically reignite our power by letting go of isolation becoming part of a greater humanity.

It should come as no surprise that feelings of joy activate our social engagement nervous system (as a recap: the ventral vagal branch of the parasympathetic nervous system innervates the head, neck, and face and is the fastest way to turn on our relaxation response). It's through our smiles, the crinkles in the corners of our eyes, and the movement of our throat muscles that this nervous system is regulated. When feeling joy, the chemical messenger in our brains, the neurotransmitter gamma-aminobutyric acid (GABA), is released. It reduces the number of signals firing in our brains. As a result, it calms our brain activity, which may lead to improved sleep, relief from anxiety, and happier moods. It also organizes the sensory processing of our nerves and reduces our blood pressure. GABA is an important piece in regulating our stress response, anxiety, and fear, and most people can create more of it simply by celebrating in the joy of others.

As you recall the good things that happened to your beloved, you may feel closer to them and you'll release oxytocin, also known as the love hormone. Research has linked oxytocin release to an increase in feeling satisfied with life.[24] Additionally, you release serotonin, a neuro-transmitter known as the feel-good chemical, which supports us by stabilizing our mood. If you find the joy exercises in this chapter to be pleasurable, then your body will also release dopamine, which is the brain's reward hormone that enhances feelings of well-being, among many other functions. The dopamine release will motivate you to engage in remembering all the good things about your loved ones more often. By engaging in the regular practice of joy, you are reigniting your power by changing your brain chemistry and choosing to experience a brighter and happier time for yourself.

Sometimes we struggle to experience joy in this bleak world because we are at a particularly challenging time in life or the devastation of the world around us seems too great, or maybe we're supporting others through a difficult time. At these moments, it feels like the joy may have vanished from your heart and left it barren. During these challenging times, finding the smallest drop of joy can help you come out of the difficult situation so that you can support your beloved, friends, family, or community. Finding time for gentle movement like dance or singing, even sad songs, can help give an authentic expression to the grief inside and allow it to release. Sometimes the best place to start is by seeking experiences that speak to that mischievous inner child that lives within us all.

Being authentic and true to your feelings is the necessary first step to move toward joy. Joy cannot be faked inside your heart. If you are hurting, then you can engage physically in joyful activities, but your heart may not join you. After expressing your genuine feelings, whether through a good cry or marching in a protest, then over time you can come back to the sympathetic joy practice of rejoicing in the goodness of others.

☪ Mindfulness Tool: Identifying Joy-Generating Activities

Now you are taking a forward-looking approach to finding experiences in your life that can create more joy within. In the first Mindfulness Tool of this chapter, I encouraged you to first grab your journal and identify activities that have brought you joy and to remember the joyful moments you've experienced with others.

Now, read through the following list, borrowing some of these ideas that make you smile, and add them to your own list of things that bring you joy. Finally, commit to incorporating joy-generating activities into your daily life.

- Relax at home while thinking of the good things happening to your beloved, your friends, your family, your community, your country, or the planet.

- Care for someone in need by giving them your undivided attention, love, time, food, or resources.

- Work in a soup kitchen and see people enjoy the food you helped prepare.

- Learn something new and enjoy the novelty of the new information.

- Spend time in nature by going for a hike, hugging a tree, letting your feet touch the bare ground, or getting wet in the rain.

- Try a new form of exercise.

- Look at the images of outer space on the NASA website and feel a sense of awe at the vast universe that you are a part of.

- Visit or see images of majestic landscapes like the incredible Antelope Canyon or Grand Canyon in Arizona, the majestic Iguazu Falls in Latin America, or the pristine Himalayan peaks in Tibet. Feel the awe and wonder of nature.

- Read a new poem every evening and notice how it makes you feel.
- Slowly savor a piece of quality chocolate, letting it melt in your mouth.
- Gather your favorite fun friends for a meal and game night.
- Create a new experience with your beloved.
- Sing or dance in a group or alone.
- Chant a mantra you are drawn to in your spiritual practice. Or just slowly repeat the word "love" and harmonize the chanting with your breath, feeling the vibration of love in your heart.

The Journey of Joy

How will you know if your practice of joy has helped you shift into your social engagement nervous system? One way is that you'll find it easier to appreciate so many of the small things in your life. You may also find that the quality of your relationships improve and feel more meaningful. When you feel the sensation of joy, you may notice that your breathing and heartbeat become faster and your body feels warmer. Unlike the racing heart of a trauma-related fight or flight response, this feeling is the healthy sympathetic response in your social engagement nervous system and will make you more resilient to stress.

Beside the nervous system regulation, I enjoy the strong feeling of contentment that washes over me when I have engaged in joyful activities. I feel more satisfied with my relationships and content with my life. There is a strong sense of meaning and purpose that guides my life when I engage in joyful activities. Maybe you can try this and see if you too feel more content. With this level of contentment, you are more likely to naturally desire to treat yourself well and engage in self-care activities. While self-care behaviors can be difficult for some of us to practice due to our environment or upbringing, the daily dose of joy practice may lead you to be gentler and more compassionate with yourself. That would be such a relief!

Equanimity for a Balanced Heart and Mind

The traditional image for equanimity is a banquet to which everyone is invited. That means that everyone and everything, without exception, is on the guest list. Consider your worst enemy. Consider someone who would do you harm. Imagine inviting them to this feast.

—Pema Chödrön

Do you remember a time when you were in the midst of a conflict with a friend, family member, or your beloved, and you were able to see where the other person was coming from? With a calm and steady mind, it is likely that you found a solution that worked for both of you. Do you recall a great loss or trauma in your past, and yet you found a calm inner center of quiet spaciousness? Do you have an experience when you were able to see the futility of a situation, and you were able to let it go with ease? At times like these, you've accessed your innate ability to meet reality with a sense of balance, stability, poise, and ease.

Equanimity (*upekkha*), the fourth Sublime State in Buddhism, is one of the most essential qualities of heart and mind because it helps you face the daily life stressors and even life-changing trauma with balance. It is defined as an even-keeled inner balance of your heart and mind, which helps you face times of loss, heartbreak, and conflict with calm equipoise and composure. It is our ability to access our innate patience and wisdom and to see with the understanding eyes of a grandmother. You may not be a grandmother, but perhaps you've had a grandmother and experienced her love. Due to her experience with the shenanigans of her own children, a grandmother does not get worried or distressed about her grandchildren's lives. This stereotypical grandma dearly loves her grandkids but is not quick to make judgments and takes time for a mindful pause to notice and reflect before offering her opinion or taking any action. If this is not your experience with your grandmother, then simply substitute someone who has been a good mentor, teacher, or life coach to you.

While our sense of loving-kindness and compassion may inspire us to want to help others, it is our equanimity that helps us to support others in a sustainable way. My client Liv learned this firsthand as she found that her dreams of opening a healing center were out of balance with the current happenings in her life.

Liv was a highly talented therapist who was strongly grounded and present in her work. At the same time, she had a powerful ability to vision—entering dreamlike states to gather wisdom for her future goals. Liv worked diligently on her inner work with the vision of someday opening a healing center for others. She loved to spend time dreaming of this center and found that her dream time helped her discover new insights and inspirations for what it would look like and what services it would offer. But, she found herself struggling with devoting time to making her center a reality while also working full time as a therapist and supporting her wife and two teenage children.

Then Liv suffered an accident that left her with severe vertigo. The dizziness left her feeling nauseated and she had difficulty sleeping. This was the forced break that Liv didn't know she needed. First, she reduced the number of clients she saw at work. Then, as we began to work through the PTSD of her accident, she realized she had to take a break from discussing her healing center during our sessions and her dreams were put on hold as well. In that time, when she was willing to pause many aspects of her life, she found that she had a deep well of inner patience and spaciousness that she didn't know existed within her.

Liv realized that she did not have to pursue everything in her life at such a frantic speed. Equanimity taught her that life is about rolling with the punches. She began showing herself compassion while she healed, finding a new balance in working with her clients, and making the best of difficult situations, like her persistent sleeplessness. During those sleepless times is when she would allow herself to re-enter the visioning realm and gather more information about her healing center. She moved through her challenges with love, grace, and patience.

Understanding Equanimity

Among all the mindfulness practices, I find equanimity to be the most difficult. Unlike loving-kindness, compassion, or joy, where your heart leads the way, equanimity requires a keen listening, understanding, and balancing of your heart. Before we can embody equanimity, let's first explore the qualities of your vast, equanimous mind and heart. You have an innate ability to meet reality with equanimity, which means that you embody these qualities:

- **Calm, clear, even mind:** With equanimity, you access a calm and clear mind, which helps you see the bigger picture and have clarity on which activities give meaning and purpose to your life. This allows you to prioritize your needs and seek support when your plate feels too full.

- **Peaceful, loving heart:** Equanimity is imbued with your love and kindness. Making decisions from a state of equanimity means choosing the most loving response for yourself and others with the intention of bringing greater harmony in the relationship.

This may come in the form of setting better boundaries that honor your needs while respecting the clarity in relationships that others desire.

- **Self-compassion:** Equanimity is imbued with compassion for yourself and others. Having the ability to know your own limitations and challenges is essential, particularly if you're engaged in social justice work, so that you can balance care for others with your self-care and self-compassion. Giving yourself permission to tap out *before* you are burned out helps to ensure you'll have longevity in the work you love.

- **Perspective:** Equanimity is your ability to have a flexible mind, which can hold different points of view. This helps you bring together opposing viewpoints and find a win-win solution. You may find that you dread conflict less as you become more adept at finding balanced solutions that meet the needs of both parties.

- **Spaciousness:** Equanimity brings a sense of ease, balance, and deliberation to your decision. When making any big decision like purchasing a property or choosing a career or a life partner, accessing this spacious quality of your mind is helpful so that your choice aligns with your values to bring balance, stability, and ease over time.

- **Taking life in stride:** Equanimity gives you the ability to accept things as they are. You know that life situations always change, if you give them some time. Difficult times almost certainly will pass. Good times pass too. That's just how life flows. Equanimity is this inner realization of change being the only thing that's permanent.

- **Enjoying celebration:** Equanimity is imbued with sympathetic joy. When you are feeling secure in your own successes and strengths, then you're more open to celebrating and enjoying the successes of others. Your body doesn't know if it is the celebration of your own achievements or that of others. Your relaxation response turns on indiscriminately when you are having a good time.

- **Values-based and heart-based action:** Equanimity is infused with loving-kindness and compassion that not only empathizes with the suffering of others but is inspired to take action too. Values- and heart-based social justice is grounded in this loving-kindness and compassion, as was the case with the founding of Mothers Against Drunk Driving (MADD). Their actions arose from their loss and grief but were grounded in equanimity and have served to benefit the safety of us all.

❀ Mindfulness Tool: How to Develop Equanimity

Let's explore ways in which you can bring equanimity to the surface so that it is present with you as you face difficult circumstances in your daily life. Remember a time when you were equanimous: You made a difficult decision and it was balanced, fair, and just. Keeping that time in mind will help you see which qualities you can develop. Now, bring to mind a situation you are in currently and journal along as you read this section:

1. **Timeline:** When you are equanimous, you are grounded in the present moment and your decisions are not influenced by past experiences and future fears. As best as you are able, notice the influence of the fearful future and past failures.

2. **Well-being:** When you are relaxed and in the present moment, you're able to enjoy small things in life like meals, tea, the moonrise, sunsets, and the dance of squirrels. Notice if this helps you to develop a sense of well-being. As you are more in the relaxed parasympathetic nervous system, does that deepen your equanimity?

3. **Open to all views:** Seeing all perspectives and challenging your own beliefs is essential in building equanimity. Sometimes this openness will bring forth a new solution to the situation. What new perspectives can you open to?

4. **Win-win:** Equanimity attempts to bring in a solution that is beneficial to all the parties concerned so there's no competition or winner-takes-all attitude. To take in other people's perspective into consideration, keenly listening to others without judgment is essential. What gets in the way of arriving at a win-win solution? If feelings of scarcity or competition are getting in the way, how can you let go of those feelings just for a few moments?

5. **Grounded in values:** When you are grounded in values such as honesty, integrity, truth, equity, and justice, then you develop faith, confidence, or conviction in your ability to engage with life and face the challenges that may arise. What are your values that you hold dear to your heart? If faced with issues of social justice or climate crisis, what values are non-negotiable?

6. **Bigger perspective:** An equanimous heart is influenced by love, compassion, and sympathetic joy. You hold a wider perspective where you can see that this situation is not just specific to you; several people on this planet may be going through it too. What larger perspective can you hold so that you feel connected to the greater humanity? How does the truth of impermanence, which says that all things will change and pass, help you see a wider view of your situation?

7. **Acceptance:** When you remember that you were unable to change past difficult situations, nor were you able to change the people, then a deep understanding and acceptance arises within. You learn to be tender and gentle with yourself when your heart contracts. You remain balanced in your thoughts and don't take things personally. What can you do to understand

that other people are responsible for their own decisions? That might include wishing them the best without taking on responsibility for their well-being. How does this process of acceptance help you understand the suffering of your loved ones and other people?

8. **Letting go:** Whether it is painful memories from the past or difficult people who have hurt you, letting go of this old pain opens a new door and you taste deeper equanimity and greater freedom. With this journaling practice complete, how does your heart feel? What sort of emotions are you experiencing?

Using Equanimity to Work with Trauma

Equanimity reminds us to stay level in the face of adversity. It's as if you're watching a butterfly struggle to break free from its chrysalis. You do not help the butterfly by freeing it from its current state of struggle. In fact, the butterfly needs that resistance to build the strength of its wings. The pressure of the chrysalis sends fluid from the butterfly's body into the wing veins. This is what allows the butterfly's wings to fully expand. You do no favors to the butterfly by robbing them of this experience.

In the time when your loved one is hurting, holding them in love and compassion is a first step toward practicing your own inner balance. Even though it may seem obvious, the knowledge that ultimately we cannot make someone else happy helps us to balance our own mind and heart. You can be loving toward them and wish them well while being mindful of your own reactions and decisions. In these situations, remind yourself that they are on their own journey and that you can't end their pain and suffering. Keep a balanced mind and heart so that when they lean on you, then you can offer them loving and compassionate support. Once you have had sufficient practice with equanimity with your loved one, then you can expand and call upon your heart to be equanimous with other challenges in life. Your equanimous heart can be indiscriminately equanimous in all situations.

The challenge with trauma is that it often leaves people feeling stuck. You can get trapped in a loop of your own nervous system because you never see the off-ramp or way out. The first section of this book offered ways to calm your nervous system. Those nervous system calming exercises combined with the practice of equanimity helps you create new neural pathways out of our habitual traumatic responses of fight, flight, or freeze. Equanimity with others means giving up control of others or trying to control their outcome. Equanimity for ourselves is the opposite. It means exploring our options and choosing the optimal path forward, even in the face of adversity. My friend Gail has a fascinating life story that illustrates how she was able to use her equanimous mind and heart to traverse some extreme challenges.

Gail was no stranger to hard work. As a young woman, she traveled for a year in a caravan of army trucks from Switzerland to South Africa, carrying food supplies for sixteen people and sufficient gas for the journey. Gail did not shy away from volunteering for challenging work, like guarding supplies at night or physically pushing the truck on plates to move it out of soft sand. Though the team leader was traveling with his girlfriend on this caravan, he began flirting with Gail. She refused his advances. He retaliated by spreading false rumors to the rest of the caravan, accusing her of not carrying her fair share of the work.

As this behavior was not aligned with Gail's values of truth and honesty, she packed her bag and left the caravan. Without a second thought, she went off alone in the middle of Africa. She had enough self-love to opt out of being subjected to such treatment. The next day, the team leader's girlfriend contacted Gail and begged her to return. She knew how much Gail contributed to the group. Gail evaluated her options and realized that she did truly wish to continue with the caravan. In order to honor herself and her values, however, she demanded that the team leader apologize before the rest of the caravan and set the record straight. He did and she continued on with her travels.

Eventually the caravan reached Mount Kilimanjaro. The sixteen caravan passengers had the opportunity to climb the mountain. Climbing this mountain was one of Gail's dreams, but she lacked the funds to hire a tour company. Undeterred, Gail evaluated her options and realized that she had the strength and tenacity to make the climb herself. Growing up in San Francisco, Gail was no stranger to long treks uphill. She believed in her ability to face the challenge.

Along the way, groups of trekkers made fun of her for her slow pace. They had the finances to hire extra guides who carried their belongings, and as they passed Gail, they made fun of her for carrying everything on her back while her guide walked beside her. Gail remained level-headed in the face of their taunts, carrying on slowly and steadily with a focus on her goal. She couldn't bring herself to strain her hired helper, so she silently bore the insults. As the air thinned and the temperatures dropped, more hikers gave in to the challenge. At that point, they applauded Gail's tenacity and even shared some of their warm clothes with her as she passed them slowly, stepping one foot in front of the other. When she reached the top, she was full of gratitude for her ability to remain calm in the face of adversity to reach her goals.

———————

Gail could have quit many times, but she would have missed out on a major dream of hers. Instead, she used her equanimity and the fact that she was clear on her values of truth, honesty, and hard work to meet challenges with a calm assertiveness. In the end, her presence not only helped with the success of her caravan group but also inspired others up the challenging climb of Kilimanjaro.

When you are grounded in your values and have the inner knowing of what they are about and what is important to you, then—like Gail—you are not affected by the criticism of others. That's perfect equanimity: You know when to fight and defend yourself, and when to not engage and focus on yourself. There is an inner knowing with equanimity that keeps you grounded, secure in yourself, and yet open-hearted and caring for others.

Working with Trauma Using Equanimity

Equanimity can have its own challenges. Of the Buddhist personalities, Peacemaker (Deluded) types often fare best with equanimity as they are most likely to see situations from various perspectives. At the same time, they may struggle with taking decisive action in the direction that is best for them. Meanwhile, Optimist (Greed) types and Strategist (Aversive) types may feel too pulled toward the positive or the negative to stay balanced in the midst of the options available to them.

The far enemy or opposite of equanimity is greed or anxiety. When we feel that we do not have enough or we are overly concerned about the path to take and feel frozen in indecision, we are experiencing the direct opposite of equanimity. We do not care about what is best for the whole but are fearful that we will be in lack or will suffer. We are overly attached to the outcome and what it means for us.

We may think that moving into a state of detachment from the outcome is moving us closer to a state of equanimity, but we could also be falling for its near enemy, indifference, which resembles equanimity. It may be difficult at first to tell if you're in a state of equanimity or indifference until you learn the key differentiators. Equanimity is always rooted in love. Indifference is rooted in fear with a closed heart. Equanimity is being present with what is. Indifference is disengagement or withdrawal from the situation. Equanimity often leads to solutions that feel like the right thing to your soul, whereas indifference leaves situations feeling unresolved and may leave you with a hollow feeling.

The near enemy of equanimity may also appear as dissociation or disconnecting from the present. I have found this in moments of sitting in comfortable meditation where my mind will float into day-dreaming or get lost in one of my own stories. In those moments I am not being present with myself, my body, and my surroundings. While it's okay to have these moments of mental disconnect or wandering, they are not indicative of us being in an equanimous meditative state.

The even-mindedness and loving state of equanimity may feel like a real challenge to access when our lives have been torn apart by personal trauma. Our personal pain can be magnified by the challenges and uncertainties of the modern era, and it is very easy for despair and pessimism to dominate our outlook. The news brings us face to face with global issues such as climate crisis, social and economic inequality, and geopolitical tensions, which cast a shadow on our collective aspirations and unbalance us. Our brain's negativity bias works against us, and soon we are doom-scrolling on social media or watching late night news to self-soothe or just numb ourselves out.

For us to counter these negative forces, it is more important than ever to identify realistic reasons for why hope and optimism will prevail in the future. If we want to be in a state of equanimity to meet these challenges with a calm, spacious, open heart, then we need to keep our focus on strengthening and building resilience in our nervous system. One way we can do this is through identifying realistic reasons to be hopeful about the future on a personal and collective level.

Think about the situations in your life that cause you worry. Where do you struggle to maintain equanimity? Now think back to when you've been in a similar situation in the past. Were you able to work through the challenge, whether that be heartbreak, fear, or betrayal? Are you able to find positive examples to counter negative worries, like the work of climate activists in the face of climate crisis?

Equanimity in Our Nervous System

Equanimity is an embodiment of the loving-kindness, compassion, sympathetic joy, or joy you feel for others. It is an embodiment of the social engagement nervous system where you feel connected to others; feel safe with others in your environment; and feel curious, playful, and creative. A characteristic of equanimity is a resilient nervous system that may go into a stress response but returns to homeostasis easily and quickly.

We often depict equanimity as being unmoved by the ups and downs of life, balanced in the midst of the turmoil of life. The nervous system of such a person will still respond to stress and threat with a sympathetic charge, but they have found an inner way of balancing their autonomic nervous system. For example, a good tennis player may lose a tournament and feel disappointment for losing the game. After taking a break, though, they get back into practice and work on improving their game. Their loss doesn't mean they aren't cut out for the sport. It's simply a setback.

Equanimity can be challenging to identify in others because it resembles other states of being. For example, some people may look very calm with very little emotion showing on their face, but they are actually in a freeze state. They may appear calm when facing an angry boss, but internally they may be shutting down even more. Sometimes meditators go into a space where they dissociate from their emotions, or they may not feel their intense emotions such as anger or rage because these emotions are not accepted as appropriate for a good meditator. Due to this distancing from their real emotions, they may be perceived as calm while internally they are having a stress response. This kind of suppression of your true emotions is not equanimity. Freeze dissociation should be worked on with a therapist to help release the bound-up energy in freeze or suppressed anger or rage.

☙ Mindfulness Tool: Inner Smile

Do you want to signal to your nervous system that everything is okay around you and that you are safe? Smile! When you smile, your brain releases hormones like dopamine, serotonin, and endorphins (the feel-good hormones), contributing to feelings of happiness and reducing stress levels. Tricking your nervous system into relaxation with an inner smile is a good hack to practice during the day. Meditators are often advised to place a gentle smile on their face when they meditate because it makes it easier to tame the mind during meditation.

Start by slightly curling your lips upward so there is a gentle smile on your face. Crinkle the corners of your eyes so that your eyes become small like they do when you genuinely smile. I realize that I am asking you to fake a smile, but by including the right elements, you may be able to trick your brain and body. After a few moments, notice if your breath becomes easier and deeper. Does your belly relax? Does your body relax? Does your brain relax? Does your stress response decrease?

You may feel strange walking around with a fake smile, so imagine this smile is in your heart and is radiating to your face and your belly. You will naturally feel your face soften and your body relax with the inner smile. This practice is tried and tested as it comes from ancient traditions like Taoism, Qigong, and *samadhi* meditation. It's even good to practice your inner smile when you are working. Try it and see if the same tasks feel easier and your stress levels are lower with an inner smile.

The Journey of Equanimity

Throughout this book you have seen the image of a pristine lotus. The lotus is revered for its beauty, grace, and resiliency as it rises above the mud, unsullied by it. Equanimity, like the lotus, arises from the transmutation of the difficult experiences of our life and is imbued with loving-kindness, compassion, and joy in the happiness of others. Just like the lotus, staying equanimous requires us to check and balance each of these Sublime States moment to moment.

If we experience too much self-compassion, we can fall into states of self-pity. Excessive compassion for others can sometimes result in the neglect of our own needs or establishing weak boundaries. If we seek too much joy, we may forget past traumas rather than being present with them and working through them. Equanimity balances our experience of all the Sublime States. While the other Sublime States may very clearly feel like they send our hearts into a state of expansion, equanimity is the one that sees our traumas and allows us to be with them. We heal and make peace with ourselves from this state. It is an essential part of reigniting our true inner power of *sat-chit-ananda*.

Just as a resilient lotus rises above the utter ugliness of a muddy pond, through equanimity, we can do the same with our trauma. We process what we can handle in each moment with an open and balanced heart. The result is a transmutation of our trauma into post-traumatic growth, which is as awe-inspiring as the blooming white lotus!

Relating with Life Through Gratitude

Gratitude is the open door to abundance.

—Anonymous

Lawrence Anthony was a South African conservationist known as the Elephant Whisperer. He rescued a herd of wild elephants that were about to be killed and gave them refuge on his reserve, Thula Thula. Over the years, Lawrence worked tirelessly to build trust with the traumatized elephants to create a sense of safety in this space. When he passed away suddenly in 2012, nobody told the elephants, and yet somehow they knew he was gone. The elephants traveled for twelve hours through the brush of Thula Thula to reach Lawrence's home. They stood in vigil, unmoving and mourning, for two days before dispersing. They were showing gratitude to the being who saved their lives.

Gratitude is foundational to both our well-being and our trauma recovery. I have been approached by several students asking why gratitude is not one of the Four Sublime States of Buddhism because of its many benefits and heart-opening abilities. Most people have an instinctive understanding of what gratitude is, but it can be surprisingly difficult to define. Is it an emotion? A virtue? A behavior? Indeed, gratitude can mean different things to different people in different contexts.

Unlike the Four Sublime States, which are most often internally generated and then expressed in a broad way to all, gratitude takes on different characteristics. Gratitude is the confidence in life itself. In it, we feel the same life force that pushes grass upward through cracks in the sidewalk. It invigorates our own life. Expressing and experiencing gratitude is a two-step process. First, we recognize that we are the beneficiary of something positive. This may be support when we needed it, encouraging words, or a kind and considerate gesture. Secondly, we recognize that there is an external source for this positive outcome we are the beneficiary of, whether that be a person, Buddha, Goddess, fate, Dharma, nature, Mother Earth, the weather, coincidence, serendipity, avoiding a mistake, or something else.

I view gratitude like a beautifully woven basket that holds us and supports us as we work to embody those sublime states—each practice of gratitude acts as another reed that fortifies the strength of the basket. Gratitude also helps us to cultivate other virtues, such as patience, humility, and wisdom. I love the practice of gratitude because we have the ability to find gratitude in everything.

For example, my friend Haresh is a regular practitioner of gratitude. In fact, he makes it a point to find about seven reasons to be grateful every day, and he maintains a list that adds up to 2,500 each year. He says it is easy to take goodness in our life for granted. Nowhere does it say that we are entitled to things working out easily for us.

Gratitude isn't only found in everything; it can be expressed in different ways. Psychologists have categorized three types of gratitude. The first is gratitude as an affective trait, meaning that one's overall tendency is to have a grateful disposition, like my friend Haresh. The second is gratitude as a mood, meaning that one experiences daily fluctuations in overall gratitude. The third is gratitude as an emotion, where one has a temporary feeling of gratitude that they may feel after receiving a gift or a favor from someone. Depending on your natural inclination, there are numerous methods of expressing gratitude, and the benefits are incredibly worthwhile.

In her 2016 commencement address for UC Berkeley, Facebook COO Sheryl Sandberg said, "Finding gratitude and appreciation is key to resilience. People who take the time to list things they are grateful for are happier and healthier. It turns out that counting your blessings can actually increase your blessings."[25]

Research from UC Davis supports this noting, "In an experimental comparison, those who kept gratitude journals on a weekly basis exercised more regularly, reported fewer physical symptoms, felt better about their lives as a whole, and were more optimistic about the upcoming week compared to those who recorded hassles or neutral life events."[26] Additionally they found that "a daily gratitude intervention resulted in higher reported levels of the positive states of alertness, enthusiasm, determination, attentiveness, and energy."

☸ Mindfulness Tool: Gratitude and Resilience

In this exercise, we take time to acknowledge our ancestors and their struggles. This exercise reminds us of what those before us endured for us as beneficiary of their efforts. I find that this builds not only our feelings of gratitude, but our feelings of resilience and the ability to overcome adversity.

1. Take a comfortable seat in your favorite chair. Have cup of tea or coffee with you as we go journey together into gratitude and resilience. You can do this practice each morning or as and when you feel called to it. When you are ready, begin by thinking about your ancestors. This may be your grandparents, great grandparents, aunts, uncles, or other relatives who came before you.

2. Identify their hardships. What was their struggle? Did they survive through war, natural disasters, or poverty? Did they live in a time when they were not granted the same rights or free-

doms as others? Did they suffer due to lack of access to necessary care or resources?

3. Envision their immense stories of bravery. Unless your ancestors are indigenous to the land in which you reside, they likely crossed a vast ocean to get to where you are today. They likely faced incredible hardship but still believed in a better future for themselves and their descendants.

4. Think about how their hopeful outlook is part of why they brought you into this world. See if you feel awe for their resilience. Are you grateful that they were resilient? Their blood flows through your veins, which makes you resilient.

5. Take a moment to acknowledge your own resilience.

How Gratitude Supports Trauma Healing

Gratitude does not envy or compare. Gratitude is not dependent on what you have. It depends on your heart. In Tibet, the monks and nuns regularly offer prayers of gratitude for suffering, saying, "Grant that I might have enough suffering to awaken in me the deepest possible compassion and wisdom." In a perhaps less poetic way, actor Robert Downey Jr. said, "I'd like to thank my terrible childhood" when he accepted his Oscar award. He was grateful for a father who started his drug addiction, with which he struggled all his life. To reach a point where you are grateful for your trauma is a sign of post-traumatic growth and also the power of gratitude to change your perspective on a twisted but unchangeable past.

How can gratitude do this? It turns out that the practice of gratitude can have a direct impact on our nervous system. Remember that if our brain stem is activated into fight, flight, or freeze mode, we may lose ourselves in survival consciousness. The reptilian brain takes charge and the neocortex is limited to rehashing the past. Tidal waves of worries may swamp our thoughts about what lies ahead. In difficult times, these tides of angst and fear can flow back and forth between one group and another. We wonder, are things getting worse or are they simply getting uncovered? And how can we respond?

You can start by tuning into your heart, where love, wisdom, grace, and compassion reside. With loving attention, begin to feel into what matters most to you. Yes, there are anxious thoughts, grief, and trauma, but don't let your heart be colonized by fear. Take time to quiet the mind and tend to the heart. Go out and look at the sky. Breathe in and open yourself to the vastness of space. Sense the seasons turning, the rise and fall of tides, the passing of dynasties and eras. Breathe out and dwell in loving awareness. Practice equanimity and steadiness. Learn from the trees. Become the still point in the center of it all. Then step toward difficulty with courage and love, and touch pain with healing rather than fear.

You can even find gratitude for your measure of sorrow, the hand you've been dealt. There is mystery surrounding even your difficulties and suffering. Sometimes it's through the hardest things that your heart learns its most important lessons. A betrayal in a relationship, whether from a business partner, family member, or beloved, may start you on a path to greater vulnerability and opening to your authentic self. I can share from personal experience that gratitude for such betrayal doesn't come easily, but it can help you open your heart to healing.

From a scientific standpoint, when we experience traumatic incidents in our lives (or an accumulation of repeated similar incidents), the strength of the corresponding emotional quotient turns on a survival center in our brains, the amygdala. Because the experience was painful, the activation of the amygdala serves to protect us from the situation happening again. In other words, it's an unconscious response to an external situation designed for self-preservation.

The more times you experience the trauma, or revisit the suffering caused by it, your amygdala and other brain areas set themselves to a new baseline. This baseline is one that is not connected to love, joy, balance, or homeostasis. Instead, it's based on the hormones of stress. If your senses are always sweeping the environment to determine if you're safe, you may find these same feelings from the past coming back in anticipation of the event happening again in the future. This subconscious mechanism is an evolutionary trait that enables us to adapt to, or at least deal with, the trauma that knocked us out of balance.

So, what is the power of love and how does love heal? When we truly open our hearts, let go of the past, and forgive, we reset our baseline into a more harmonious, more elevated state. This in turn brings us into a state of homeostasis, and by returning to homeostasis, we free ourselves from the past. When we free ourselves from the past, we gain a new freedom to create our future. You may be surprised at what other changes this heart opening can have in your life.

I have found that gratitude opens my heart and connects me with the divinity within me. Even in difficult times, it gives me a feeling of interconnection and support. It is a great way to reduce feelings of isolation and loneliness. And this profound sense of gratitude can arise in the simplest of ways. One of my daily practices is to show gratitude before a meal. The bonus of doing this practice is that my food tastes delicious and feels nourishing to my body.

It is interesting to take one activity, like the plate of food before you at lunch, and reflect on how you got to this moment. When I sit before my meal and reflect on how this meal got before me, I am filled with gratitude for my clients, students, and organizations who are the source of my income. I'm grateful to my Ayurvedic doctor who has painstakingly helped me make food choices in harmony with my body. I feel gratitude for all the farmers who woke up before dawn to cultivate their fields, the transportation industry and the truckers who drove in the dark of the night to bypass the interstate traffic to bring this food to grocery stores. I have gratitude for the folks at the grocery stores who cleaned the store after closing hours and stocked the groceries, and to my own body for preparing the food and heating it with delicious spices.

I am filled with gratitude toward all of them. But more so I am filled with awe that my body will convert this broccoli into blood, muscle, and tissue that creates Pawan Bareja. It really is a miracle! This amazing chemical factory in my body with its innate intelligence fills me with awe every time I sit before my meal. It makes the experience that much more satisfying. In the simple act of eating a meal, my social engagement nervous system turns on and I feel connected and supported by the many people who bring me this nurturing meal.

☸ Mindfulness Tool: How Did I End Up Here?

There is a sense of coherence and being connected with everyone when you're in gratitude. Writer and professor Bob McKinnon uses a simple question to jumpstart this awareness: "How did I end up here?"[27] Once you're in that coherent space of heart, mind, and body, then anything that is tugging at you, hurting you, or reminding you of past traumas becomes easier to let go. Forgiveness is also easier when you're in this coherent space.

1. Begin by thinking of something you're grateful for in your life. Perhaps it's the experience of tucking your children into bed or your cat curled up and purring on your lap. Perhaps it's the friend who makes you laugh, even on your difficult days. Or your dog's enthusiastic good morning greeting ritual! What is something that feels good in your heart right now that you can show gratitude for?

2. Now start to work backward to figure out how that experience you're grateful for came to be. Perhaps it's showing gratitude for your beloved, who was a part in bringing your children into this world, and your doctor or midwife who helped deliver them earthside. You might be grateful for whatever means connected

you with that medical support. You might even think back to how the relationship with your beloved first began and all of the experiences and feelings you both went through before ever reaching the point of having children.

3. As you go about your day and encounter more things that open your grateful heart, take a moment to look back with gratitude for the small steps, people, things, and actions that helped get you to where you are.

The Challenges of Gratitude

With the immense benefits of gratitude, it may be difficult to believe that gratitude can have a dark side. We have the ability to bypass our pain, create feelings of shame, or keep ourselves in bad situations because of the thought, "There is always something to be grateful for." One study found that people with disabilities who relied on informal support for their care often felt burdened by gratitude.[28] Specifically, they reported feeling forced to express gratitude in order to secure the support that they needed and expressed shame and frustration over the one-sided nature of their dependent relationships. In contrast, people with disabilities who were able to pay for formal support reported feeling more comfortable and more in control of their lives.

These challenges with gratitude extend to other areas as well. A study of survivors of dating violence suggests that survivors with more dispositional gratitude, those prone to find gratitude in most things, may work harder to maintain a relationship in which they are being abused.[29] Those with less gratitude became aware of their unmet emotional needs and were able to leave the unhealthy relationship. And, when it comes to social interactions, people who receive a large gift or favor often have a more difficult time setting appropriate relationship boundaries.[30] In the social justice realm, a lack of gratitude may be a moral response, according to Liz Jackson, associate professor of education at the University of Hong Kong.[31] According to Jackson, when we promote the idea that marginalized people (such as people of color in the U.S., manual laborers, or people in abusive partnerships) should express gratitude for what they have, it may temporarily help them from a psychological perspective. At the same time, recommending gratitude in these situations may also deny them the reality of the hardship they're facing or minimize their problems that need resolution.

The dark sides of gratitude can arise when we become grateful for our difficult life experiences and try to find the life lesson before we've actually taken the time to feel, tolerate, and embody the emotions our difficult experiences have created. In these instances, we are not actually feeling gratitude. Instead, we are using the concept of gratitude to bypass our inner work or healing. I have seen this in working with my client Erin.

Erin is a meditator who was recently betrayed by her beloved. Determined to overcome the pain, she used her spiritual practice to "rise above it all." Erin quickly dove into a gratitude practice to shield herself from fully feeling the difficult emotions of loss, crushing self-esteem, shame, and self-blame. Instead, if she were able to stay with these emotions and embody them as we've learned, then she would develop the capacity to weather the turbulence of these emotions and release them.

We can experience gratitude honestly and fully when we do so in an embodied way. When we are not in this embodied state, we may become more prone to other faux feelings of gratitude. One way we may do this is by overextending ourselves during the holidays by making donations beyond what we can really afford. It's easy to get swept up in the spirit of generosity, but if we're doing it from a place of faux generosity, thinking that it will make us feel better, we often find that we are left with guilt and regret. We come from a place of desiring gratitude and abundance but end up causing a disservice to ourselves in the process.

I was often guilty of this when I was living in India. In my teen and young adult years, there were times late at night where I would be waiting for the bus and someone would inevitably ask me for money. It was like I was a magnet for those in need. On more than one occasion I gave away my last fifty pence and no longer had money for bus fare. While that may appear generous or noble to some, my friends pointed out that this giving comes from a place of guilt. It also puts me in danger as I then have to walk through the dark streets alone at night to make my way home.

Prati, my high school friend, would spend hours arguing with me about using my head instead of my heart and would share articles of how there were rings of beggars who were trained to draw out sympathy. The reality was that some of them were, in fact, quite wealthy. This was simply an easy way for them to make money. Even today, my friends know that I am a work-in-process and haven't given up on training me. Now, when my plane lands in India they come prepared to hand me a lot of small change so that I can give money to the teeming beggar kids who surround people exiting the airport.

I have learned that my mixed messages about gratitude, combined with feelings of pity, came from my youth. They are the same feelings that my mother invoked in me when she would ask me to finish the morsels of unpalatable bitter gourd on my plate by saying, "There are hungry children in Africa." She would also say, "Clean up your plate and don't waste food!" Interestingly, these are the same lines that my friends from countries around the world also heard from their parents. With these words, my mother was attempting to remind me that I live with abundance. In doing so, however, she was invoking a feeling of guilt for my abundance of food on my plate. While her strategy was indeed successful at getting me to eat every morsel, it was not truly teaching me to live from a feeling of gratitude for what we have.

Due to our upbringing, our belief systems, or simply the way our minds and nervous systems work, we may become our own greatest barrier to experiencing true gratitude. Instead, we find ourselves with feelings of envy, materialism, narcissism, or cynicism. Our brains may be dominated by our negativity bias, so that every time we do feel gratitude it's followed by a negative thought of what is going wrong or how things could be better.

☸ Mindfulness Tool: Morning Gratitude

Knowing how our minds are wired, I like to start each day giving myself the best chances at having a day that is rooted in gratitude and heart-opening practices. Each morning, before I do much else, I practice the following gratitude exercise. I encourage you to try this for yourself and see if it transforms the tone of your day.

1. Count ten things that you are grateful for. These may be things that impact you directly, like waking up without back pain or being able to smell your morning coffee. It may also be gratitude in a broad sense, like having a rainstorm in your town after a long period of drought.

2. Then write these experiences and feelings of gratitude in a gratitude journal. Not only does this help solidify your thoughts in the moment and adds a tactile experience through writing, but now you have a beautiful collection of all the wondrous happenings in your life to look back on.

3. Finally, think of a benefactor who has supported you and see if you feel grateful to them. It may be a teacher from your past who helped you get the career of your dreams or that friend who gave you an unexpected hug when you needed it most. This final step reminds you of your interconnectedness with others and taps into your social engagement nervous system.

Living in Gratitude

Gratitude enables our heart to reside in loving-kindness, compassion, joy, and equanimity in the midst of life's challenges. At the end of life, no one wishes they had bought nicer things or read more social media posts. Even in our fast-paced, goal-driven lives, we can strive for meaningful connection with ourselves and others. The simple practice of gratitude can awaken us to the outrageous beauty of life force already pulsing all around us.

Gratitude is an antidote to our mind's fear, opening the door to humility, reverence, and even devotion. It can permeate our deepest fears, from eco-anxiety to sickness and loss. With gratitude and awe, we feel the wonder and connection to the Earth and all beings, meeting the world with the energy to transform and accept what is needed.

Reigniting Your Power with Forgiveness

Holding on to anger is like grasping a hot coal with the intent of throwing it at someone else; you are the one who gets burned.

—Buddha

How do people forgive when the unforgivable has happened? I often think of my ancestors in India, those subjected to a brutal rule under the British Empire that robbed them of their resources, their freedoms, and their way of life. When I was a teenager, studying the history of my country, I found myself wondering how some Indian leaders who worked for India's independence from the British did so through dialogue, rather than violence. What must their hearts have felt like to rise above the atrocities they witnessed every day?

When I think about forgiveness, my mind also goes to Nelson Mandela, the Black South African activist who was imprisoned under apartheid for twenty-seven years. During those many years, the guards outside his cell were changed regularly because he would talk to them and they would come to love him so much that there was a risk they would release him. Mandela lived with an open heart and the ability to forgive. He was even able to forgive, befriend, and love those who sentenced him to so many years apart from his wife and friends. It is no wonder that Mandela served as South Africa's first Black president and was able to bring much-needed healing to his country's racial divide. That is the power of forgiveness!

You may be surprised to know that I rarely teach anything related to forgiveness in my classes on trauma healing. From my perspective, forgiveness is something that is mostly unteachable. There are no words I can share with you, no exercises I can design for you, no amount of desire in my heart that I can have that will grant you the experience of forgiveness. True forgiveness is a release of the pain from your tender and vulnerable heart. It is a state of being that can only be deeply felt when you realize that at the beginning and at the end (of this book and in life) it is all about love. It's about your open heart!

So then why write a chapter on forgiveness with stories, exercises, and statistics? I believe it is necessary because you must know that forgiveness is possible and is something that you can work toward by sowing seeds of loving-kindness, compassion, joy, equanimity, and gratitude in the garden of your heart. Forgiveness may not always be perfect, but it is attainable and a part of healing from trauma.

That first step toward forgiveness means checking in with yourself and the state of your heart. Is it open or closed? This is not something someone else can identify for you. Through introspection you can see if you're afraid to open to new experiences of life. If so, you may realize that you are imprisoned by your own pain, anger, and resentment. When you are ready to reclaim your love and your ability to love, to be spontaneous, and to care for others, that means you are ready to break out of the prison, and you will naturally move toward forgiveness.

In the dictionary, *forgive* is defined as "to give up resentment against or the desire to punish; stop being angry with; pardon." Psychologists generally define forgiveness as a conscious, deliberate decision to release feelings of resentment or vengeance toward a person or group who has harmed you, regardless of whether they actually deserve your forgiveness. Just as important as defining what forgiveness is, though, is understanding what forgiveness is not. Forgiveness does not mean forgetting, nor does it mean condoning or excusing offenses. Forgiveness is also about boundaries. It allows you to let go and also take measures to prevent the same transgression from occurring in the future. Experts on forgiveness make clear that when you forgive, you do not gloss over nor deny the seriousness of an offense against you. Though forgiveness can help repair a damaged relationship, it doesn't obligate you to reconcile with the person who harmed you or release them from legal accountability.

Instead, forgiveness brings us peace of mind and frees us from corrosive anger. Forgiveness frees us from the mental loop of reliving and reprocessing whatever traumatic event we experienced. My friend once described forgiveness as being able to see someone's betrayal as a bad nightmare rather than our present experience. Like a nightmare that is an illusion of our mind, she said, it happened in the past and doesn't have to filter into the present. She would encourage us to let that person go or to let that experience go. Letting go of a deeply held painful past empowers you to recognize the pain you suffered without letting that pain define you, enabling you to heal and move on with your life. In this way, forgiveness is an essential part of trauma healing. But it cannot be forced. It happens when the right conditions come together within your heart, and your heart surrenders and releases the past.

Forgiveness doesn't necessarily mean that you have to speak or relate to a person who betrayed you. It's not about them. It doesn't condone their behavior—it can stand up for justice and say, "no more." If trauma is like a lock, forgiveness is sometimes that key that can release you from the feelings of anger, resentment, or hate and open our hearts to feel more loving-kindness, compassion, joy, and equanimity. An example of this is my client Sofia.

———————

Sofia was in her twenties when she met Ben. While things were far from perfect, Sofia deeply loved him and he loved her. At some point in the relationship, though, Ben began to get into drugs, which caused their relationship to deteriorate. Ben also began cheating on Sofia with several other women. It became too much for her heart and her boundaries. Finally, Sofia left him.

Ben continued to pursue Sofia for twenty years after their relationship ended. It was too late. Her heart was closed off to him. She felt hatred toward the other women that Ben cheated with. Then, Ben died. Sofia had many emotions to process around his death, including grief associated with what was and what could have been in their relationship.

Processing grief did not open Sofia's heart, though. For that, she needed to forgive Ben and the other women, even though having a conversation with them in person was not a possibility. As she worked through her forgiveness, Sofia could feel the effects of her heart reopening. She began to move through life with more joy and vulnerability. This changed the way that others in her world interacted with her, with a more open heart.

———

Sofia had many complicated emotions to work through due to her relationship with Ben and then his passing. Sometimes the forgiveness that is needed to free our heart is not in forgiving our beloved, family, friends, community, or business partner. Instead, it involves forgiving ourselves. That was the final heart opening for Sofia as she forgave herself and let go self-judgment over wasted years of her youth. Her heart opened naturally as she was able to release her past.

Sometimes, especially after illness, we need to forgive our body for letting us down. My dear friend and fellow author Nil Demircubuk wrote the most touching poem about pain and forgiveness and how she came to accept her own body, and she's allowed me to share it with you here. In her mid-thirties, a few years after she successfully completed her PhD, her health forced her to leave her corporate job with a financial tech company when she was at the peak of her career. The poem is a beautiful illustration of how the practice of forgiveness impacts more than just our mind and our heart; it opens us into the mystery of life.

The Mirror

How could the memory
And the image of the perfect
Person I was trying to be
Shatter in pieces so easily?
I cannot even look at
The mirror anymore.
I cannot seem to forget
All the pain, the misery
This long fight has cost me.
I just see eyes so heavy,
Full of tears that cannot flow,
A throat so tight
Full of words it had to swallow,
And a body so tired
It cannot even stand straight.
Then I see my true self.
When I look deep inside
I see my soul shining through.
Full of love and hope
Once again coming to the rescue.
And the tears start flowing,
I see butterflies of light
Flying around me glowing,
Telling me that I am not alone.
My tears melt the words
Stuck in my throat
And the pain sunk in my chest.
They pour out onto the paper,
Disappear into the air.
The phone still does not ring.

No one knows that I've been crying.
And I start feeling
Much lighter than before
As I realize that in this game,
This life that we live,
There is no one to blame
But so much to forgive.

As Nil's poem illustrates, forgiveness can take us to the next level in our heart practice through connection rather than desolation and loneliness. It not only heals the mind but can be beneficial to our health in many ways. Research studies have found the following benefits to our well-being when we experience feelings of forgiveness:

- **Reduced stress:**[32] When we dwell on past wrongs, our blood pressure and heart rate spike—signs of stress that damage the body. When we forgive, our stress levels drop, and people who are more forgiving are protected from the negative health effects of stress, including compromised immune systems.

- **Improved mental health:**[33] People who receive therapy designed to foster forgiveness experience greater improvements in depression, anxiety, and hope than those who don't. They are also at a decreased risk of suicide.

- **Greater happiness:**[34] Research suggests not only that happy people are more likely to forgive but that forgiving others can make people feel happy, especially when they forgive someone with whom they feel close.

- **Improved social bonds:**[35] In relationships, studies suggest that forgiveness can stop downward spirals and repair our relationships before they dissolve.

- **Increased kindness and connectedness:**[36] People who feel forgiving don't only feel more positive toward someone who hurt them, they are also more likely to want to volunteer and donate money to charity, and they feel more connected to other people in general.

These benefits have extended to some of the most traumatic relationships, like that between the Tutsis and Hutus in Rwanda. A research-based forgiveness training program in Rwanda found that the Tutsi and Hutu who participated in the program experienced reduced trauma and more positive attitudes.[37] A study of people who learned forgiveness skills in war-torn Sierra Leone found that they reported feeling less depressed, more grateful, more satisfied with life, and less stressed afterward. Perhaps most famously, South Africa's Truth and Reconciliation Commission is widely credited with encouraging forgiveness and reconciliation after the end of apartheid in that country. Archbishop Desmond Tutu, the commission's chairman, argued that forgiveness is the path to "true enduring peace."[38] When we choose not to forgive, we are choosing a disservice to ourselves.

⚘ Mindfulness Tool: Acknowledging Past Forgiveness

When we acknowledge our past, we can strengthen our forgiveness practice. This exercise is to help you become conscious of the qualities of your heart and mind that fueled your forgiveness practice. The goal is to bring awareness to the contraction in your heart and the release and freedom, as in Nil's poem.

1. Begin by thinking of one difficult situation where you had difficulty forgiving either your own self or another person, but, in the end, you did forgive!

2. Then, think about how you were able to forgive. Determine why you decided to forgive and let go.

3. Remember how contracted your heart and mind were when you did not forgive and the release after forgiveness. Remember how imprisoning it felt to be gripped by the hurt, pain, and betrayal and how freeing it currently feels after letting go.

Choosing Forgiveness

Given some of the horrible and traumatizing situations that have occurred around the world, how is it that people are still able to find forgiveness in their hearts? What is it that allows us to forgive with relative ease at some times, while other times forgiveness feels nearly impossible? There are several reasons that impact the ease with which we can forgive, including because there are different qualities to the experiences and how the transgressor apologizes (or doesn't). Researcher Aaron Lazare has studied apologies for years and concluded that an effective apology must have four parts:[39]

1. The apology acknowledges the offense.
2. The apology offers an explanation for the offense.
3. The apology expresses remorse or shame.
4. The apology involves a reparation of some kind.

We rarely get a complete apology. In some cases, the transgressor may not be alive or not in our life anymore. So in these unresolved situations, how do we move past our hurt? First, we must understand that the ability to forgive is not an innate characteristic that some people have and others don't. Forgiveness is a choice we make and a skill that we can strengthen.

Dr. Robert Enright, cofounder of the International Forgiveness Institute, created the Process Model of Forgiving, which includes four phases and twenty steps. The following outlines those phases, which I hope will guide you on your path to forgiveness and letting go:

1. **Uncovering Phase:** During this phase, you become aware of the emotional pain that has resulted from a deep, unjust injury. That pain may be compounded by feelings of anger or even hatred, which is called the second arrow (discussed in chapter 2). This first step is about acknowledging your emotional distress as honestly as possible so that healing can begin to occur.

2. **Decision Phase:** In this phase you have felt the pinch of holding onto the past and commit to forgive and let go. You naturally come to the realization that focusing on the injury is simply grooving deeper neural pathways in your brain and begin to understand that a change must occur to go ahead in the healing process. Your heart has had enough of the pain and wishes to live a more happy life. You just take the first step toward forgiveness with our commitment and understand that complete forgiveness is not yet realized. A difficult, yet important, aspect of this step is to forego any thoughts, feelings, or intentions of revenge toward the person who has caused you harm.

3. **Work Phase:** This is where you come to accept—but not condone—the pain you have suffered, no matter how undeserved. To help you let go, you may come to understand the causes and conditions that led to the situation or develop empathy toward the person who has caused harm. You bear your pain as consciously as possible and may choose loving-kindness meditations or offerings of goodwill to all (including your transgressor). The work phase also includes the heart of forgiveness, which lies in acceptance of your pain and may or may not include reconcilia-

tion. It may include setting boundaries so that you have a greater sense of trust and safety, and so that the painful past history isn't repeated.

4. **Outcome/Deepening Phase:** In this phase you begin to feel the emotional relief from the process of forgiving the person who has hurt you. As your heart lets go, you may find meaning in the suffering that you have faced. The open heart has a greater capacity for compassion for yourself and others. You may discover a new purpose in life and an active concern for your community. You may discover the paradox of forgiveness: as you give to others the gifts of mercy, generosity, and moral love, you yourself are healed.

These four phases represent an understanding of the general pathway that people follow when they forgive someone who has unjustly injured them.

Enright's twenty-step process is not a rigid sequence, and individuals may experience all or only some of the steps as they undertake the journey of forgiveness. In addition to outlining this step-by-step approach of how to forgive in his book *Forgiveness Is a Choice*, Dr. Enright has produced a condensed version of the process in another book, *Eight Keys to Forgiveness*. I hope these hands-on guides will be useful to you if you decide to delve deeper into self-forgiveness as well as interpersonal forgiveness.

☙ Mindfulness Tool: Finding the Freedom of Your Heart

You can use Dr. Enright's steps and the Buddhist forgiveness practice to explore a state of forgiveness with this exercise that may help you to open your heart. You will explore three types of forgiveness, thinking through incidents that caused you pain. Since you are just starting on your path of forgiveness, I suggest that you pick small transgressions to practice.

1. **Forgiving someone who has harmed you:** Start by remembering an incident where someone may have hurt you in the past. Check in to see if you still hurt, and if you are open to forgiving them and freeing your heart. Are you ready to let go of feelings of revenge? If not, then select someone else as the person you wish to forgive.

   Next, see what would help you let go of the hurt and pain. Would a deeper understanding of that person's limitations as a human being help you let go? When you are ready to let go, you can use the Buddhist phrases for forgiveness (or create your own phrases): "For any harm you may have caused me, knowingly or unknowingly, in your thoughts, words, or actions, I forgive you as best as I am able."

   See if you feel your heart release and let go a little bit. See if you breathe deeper and body relaxes. Notice if your recursive thinking reduces, a sign that the amygdala is finally relaxing.

2. **Forgiving harm you've caused someone else:** Yes, this is a difficult one to face. With your tears, pain, anger, and upset at the person who has harmed you, you can cause harm to them through your thoughts, such as cursing them or wishing they had as much pain as you do. Or you may have harmed someone else and caused them stress or pain or loss.

   In these situations, again, follow the steps of Enright's model. Thinking of yourself as a human being who is capable of behaving badly helps in self-forgiveness. When you feel ready, use the Buddhist phrases of forgiveness: "For any harm I may have caused you, knowingly or unknowingly, in my thoughts, words, or actions, I ask for your forgiveness."

3. **Forgiving harm you've caused yourself:** In my experience, this is the hardest part of forgiveness practice. We are hard on ourselves, self-critical, and drive ourselves beyond our human limits—all different forms of self-punishment. See if you are ready to give yourself the gift of mercy or compassion so that your own heart is liberated. When you are ready, you can use the Buddhist phrases as a mantra for self-forgiveness: "For any harm I may have caused myself, knowingly or unknowingly, in my thoughts, words or actions, I forgive myself as best as I am able."

Notice the use of the phrase "as best as I am able." It is a way to allow your heart to decide when to release the past hurt and not push it. As you receive the gift of forgiveness with your heart opening and maybe begin walking on your life path, I hope you will be consciously aware of the thoughts, feelings, and physical responses that arise within you as you cultivate compassion, kindness, and mercy toward yourself and the person who has harmed you.

Reigniting Your Power with Forgiveness

Throughout this book, I have shared the stories, teachings, and psychology of Buddhism. Perhaps one of the most powerful and moving stories about the Buddha in his lifetime, though, is the compassionate forgiveness he offered in his final moments. Buddha journeyed to a mango grove owned by Cunda Kammaraputta, a metalsmith. Cunda offered Buddha a meal that was believed to be either pork or mushrooms. Unfortunately, the food was tainted and Buddha found himself in tremendous pain as food poisoning ate away at his intestines. He knew he was dying.

In a final act before he passed, Buddha told Ananda, his cousin and closest monk, to visit Cunda and tell him the meal had nothing to do with him getting ill, and therefore he should feel no blame nor remorse.

On the contrary, offering the Buddha his last meal before passing to the spirit plane was equal to offering him his first meal before attaining Buddhahood. Thus, Cunda should not take this event personally and should rejoice that Buddha would soon become one with the bliss of existence.

Buddha likely had a gift of foresight, based on other occurrences in his life where he demonstrated a greater knowing. It is likely that Buddha knew in advance that his meal from Cunda would be his last. Even still, out of immense compassion, he accepted Cunda's offering, made with love, and ate it. Buddha realized the impact that his death would potentially have on Cunda and sent a message to him to pacify his mind and heart with Dharma. I know I wouldn't be able to forgive myself if I were in Cunda's shoes. Buddha, in his immense compassion, realized that and soothed Cunda's heart even as he lay on his deathbed, writhing in pain. That is an example of forgiveness coming out of an open heart, immense love, and nonattachment to one's own body.

I can say for myself that I don't have the ability to forgive at the level of the Buddha, but his example inspires me to find that kernel of forgiveness in my heart.

If you remember back to the beginning of this book and the Four Noble Truths of Buddhism, then you recall that suffering is the First Noble Truth of life. We can be hurt in ways that upend our lives. The Second Noble Truth is that our suffering is caused by our attachment or holding on. Trauma, especially major trauma, is hard to let go of and it is easy to let it take over our lives. At some point we may ask ourselves, "Am I ready to reclaim my body, my heart, and my life?" The Third Noble Truth is the end of suffering. This is where forgiveness resides, imploring us to let go of the grievous hurt that disrupts our inner world.

The Fourth Noble Truth is about following Buddhism's Eightfold Path. This path involves cultivating right understanding, right thought, right speech, right action, right livelihood, right effort, right mindfulness, and right concentration. When we are able to release that which causes our suffering, we find our life path and are able to move forward in so many areas of our lives. We hold the key to our own liberation.

Transgressions are a part of life. Conflicts and transgressions seem inevitable as humans rub against each other. The sharp corners of our personalities irritate and scuff against those with whom we interact on a daily basis. But if the new science of forgiveness has proved anything, it's that these offenses don't need to condemn us to a life of hurt and aggravation. As Elie Wiesel, the Nobel laureate and Holocaust survivor, wrote, "Suffering confers neither privileges nor rights. It all depends on how you use it. If you use it to increase the anguish of yourself or others, you are degrading, even betraying it. Yet the day will come when we shall understand that suffering can also elevate human beings. God help us to bear our suffering well."[40]

At the end of the day, you have to find what works for you when it comes to forgiveness. For me, the more I have developed loving-kindness, compassion, sympathetic joy, gratitude, and equanimity in my life, the more easily I am able to forgive. From there I can choose whether I want to hold on to some hurt or pain and create disharmony in my life. The disharmony from not forgiving ruins the harmony of my happiness. If I am spending most of my time being happy and joyful throughout the day, and my happiness is important to me, then I will find a way to release my heart and let go of the painful event. There is a momentum to happiness. Similarly, you have so many ways to open your heart within this book.

With the knowledge you have gained and the work you have done, it's time to reignite your power. It has always been inside of you. Let your power reside in your heart—where it never has and never will be lost. It is just waiting to be reignited.

Conclusion

There is no path to happiness: happiness is the path.

—Buddha

There is this belief held by some that when we go through traumatic situations, they rob us of our power—as if it is some tangible object that can be taken and returned. For my students and clients, they feel that their trauma has changed the trajectory of their lives and nervous systems, closing their hearts off from the world. We could tell ourselves the story that our power is like a golden egg that the dragon of trauma is guarding. We may convince ourselves that we are victims, somehow disrupted from our life path with the new challenge of slaying this powerful beast to reclaim what was taken from us. And when we do, peace will be restored to the kingdom.

I hope by now, dear reader, that you understand trauma in a different way. While we may envision it as a dragon or an external event, the reality is that trauma becomes part of us. There is no escaping or slaying it—but why would we want to? It happened and it shaped us. Rather than pretend it never existed, forever fearing it in our shadows, we can own it, be with it, and make peace with it. Trauma does not change our innate power of *sat-chit-ananda*, regardless of what happened. Our true nature is always there, and so is our power. In my experience, trauma leaves us with a gift, a doorway to reach our divine nature.

Buddhism's view on power has always differed from how it is often defined in Western culture. Rather than a force wielded over others or a resume full of achievements, Buddhist power is an internal event. This type of power is inner strength and stability, cultivated through practices like self-awareness and mindfulness. With this perspective, we realize that we can never *ever* be robbed of our power. It is always within us, and all we need to do is reignite it.

That is a powerful knowledge to have. Once you understand and have experienced that your power is innate and that you hold the keys to finding it and strengthening it, you realize that there is very little life can throw at you that you couldn't endure. Jack Kornfield said, "Being on a spiritual path does not prevent you from facing times of darkness. But it teaches you how to use the darkness as a tool to grow."[41] You have always had your power. Now you have the tools to reignite it and live a full life. Like a lotus in a murky pond blossoms with the sun rays each morning, you have the power within you to open to your life with aliveness, innocence, love, and kindness despite the harshness of the world. When you choose to be a lotus despite the mud, you give yourself the blessing to transmute your pain from betrayal, loss, and pain into aliveness and well-being.

But pain is only a piece of the picture. If you look at the purpose and intention of this book, it is to reclaim and reignite your power so that you can once again enjoy life. This message came to me in a dream I had about a month before I concluded the writing of the book. In that time, I had been working hard to craft what I felt were just the right words, the right stories, and the right exercises told in just the right way. Whereas in my life I try to live with lightness, I began to feel an unusual weight of responsibility with this book. That is when the Hindu god, Ganesh, came to visit me.

In the dream I was trying to read a mantra on a sign. Perhaps this was a message that needed to be in my book! And yet, every time I tried to read it, Ganesh, in his elephant form with big floppy ears, would distract me, playfully dancing in front of me. I could feel myself light up inside, filled with the energy of fun. While this book talks about working with trauma, I believe that this timely visit from Ganesh was the playful reminder that we should hold everything lightly. Because, truly, this is not actually a book about trauma; it's a book about moving beyond your trauma to reclaim your ability to dance with life. It's not about knowing the right words or having the right mantra; it's about rekindling that feeling of joy and belonging. It's about unfolding your lotus heart of love, wisdom, and compassion in the midst of the stressful and muddy waters of our daily lives, without changing our external environment. It's about removing the dust of trauma and reigniting your innate power of *sat-chit-ananda*.

And so, my dear reader, while our time together in this book may come to a close, it is my desire for you that you carry the spirit and energy of aliveness with you for the rest of your days. Working through your trauma is possible. Creating a community where you feel safe, loved, and cared for is possible. Reigniting the power that was always with you is not only possible, it is your birthright. When the anger or rage of the fight response is harnessed and directed, it becomes power. When fear or terror of the flight response is metabolized, it becomes courage to face your difficulties. When the freeze response is thawed and worked with, it shows up as greater aliveness in all aspects of your life.

You are born for love! You are love! You do not have to get anything "right" and you do not have to fix anything within you. Mindfulness is innately yours, always. You only need to choose when you desire the unfolding of your lotus heart.

With love and blessings,

Pawan

Notes

1. Gordon Ramel, "Do Peacocks Eat Snakes and How Do They Kill Them?" Earth Life, July 11, 2023.

2. "The Buddhist Peacock," Tibetan Buddhist Encyclopedia, January 6, 2024.

3. Satish K. Murari et al., "Use of Pavo cristatus feather extract for the better management of snakebites: neutralization of inflammatory reactions," *Journal of Ethnopharmacology* 99, no. 2 (2005): 229–237.

4. Peter A. Levine with Ann Frederick, *Waking the Tiger: Healing Trauma* (Berkeley, CA: North Atlantic Books, 1997).

5. Robert C. Scaer, *The Body Bears the Burden: Trauma, Dissociation, and Disease, Second Edition* (Philadelphia, PA: The Haworth Medical Press, 2001).

6. Tammi R. A. Kral, et al., "Impact of short- and long-term mindfulness meditation training on amygdala reactivity to emotional stimuli," *Neuroimage* 181 (2018): 301–13.

7. Thich Nhat Hanh, "Please Call Me by My True Names," Plum Village, June 3, 2020.

8. William R. Marchand, "Neural mechanisms of mindfulness and meditation: Evidence from neuroimaging studies," *World Journal of Radiology* 6, no. 7 (2014): 471–79.

9. James Tobin, "The Psychology of Resilience: Coping Challenges and How Psychotherapy Bolsters Adaptability," James Tobin Ph.D., September 27, 2024.

10. Isabella Helmreich, et al., "Psychological interventions for resilience enhancement in adults," *Cochrane Database of Systematic Reviews* 2 (2017): CD012527.

11. "The Importance of Resilience-Building Strategies in Therapy and Skill Development," Heartwise, April 17, 2025.

12. "Mindfulness Interventions in Physical Rehabilitation: A Scoping Review," Mark E Hardison, Shawn C Roll, *American Journal of Occupational Therapy*, 2016 Apr 1; 70(3):7003290030p1–70032900 30p9.

13. Wim Hof, *The Wim Hof Method: Activate Your Full Human Potential* (Louisville, CO: Sounds True, 2020).

14. "Key Term: Navajo Healing Ceremony," Fiveable, accessed August 19, 2025.

15. Paul D MacLean, *The Triune Brain in Evolution: Role in Paleocerebral Functions* (New York: Plenum Press, 1990).

16. Meir Schneider, *Awakening Your Power of Self-Healing* (Self-Healing Press, 2017).

17. Dan Siegel, "An Introduction to Interpersonal Neurobiology," drdan-siegel.com, accessed August 19, 2025.

18. Stephen W. Porges, *The Polyvagal Theory: Neurophysiological Foundations of Emotions, Attachment, Communication, and Self-Regulation* (New York: W. W. Norton & Company, 2011).

19. Deb Dana, *The Polyvagal Theory in Therapy: Engaging the Rhythm of Regulation* (New York: W. W. Norton & Company, 2018).

20. Jack Kornfield, *A Path with Heart: A Guide Through the Perils and Promises of Spiritual Life* (New York: Bantam, 1993).

21. Judith Joseph, *High Functioning: Overcome Your Hidden Depression and Reclaim Your Joy.* (New York: Little, Brown Spark, 2025).

22. Robert A. Johnson, *Owning Your Own Shadow: Understanding the Dark Side of the Psyche* (New York: HarperCollins, 1994).

23. Prentis Hemphill, *What It Takes to Heal: How Transforming Ourselves Can Change the World* (New York: Random House, 2024).

24. Paul Zak, Ben Curry, Tyler Owen, and Jorge Barraza, "Oxytocin Release Increases With Age and Is Associated With Life Satisfaction and Prosocial Behaviors," *Frontiers in Behavioral Neuroscience* 16 (2022): e846234; Ekaterina Schneider, et al., "Affectionate touch and diurnal oxytocin levels: An ecological momentary assessment study," *eLife* 12 (2023): e81241.

25. Sheryl Sandberg, "University of California, Berkeley, 2016 Commencement Address," May 14, 2016, Berkeley, CA, news.

26. Robert A. Emmons and Michael E. McCullough, "Counting blessings versus burdens: an experimental investigation of gratitude and subjective well-being in daily life," *Journal of Personality and Social Psychology* 84, no. 2 (2003): 377–89.

27. Bob McKinnon, *Three Little Engines* (New York: Grosset & Dunlap, 2021).

28. Rose Galvin, "Challenging the Need for Gratitude: Comparisons Between Paid and Unpaid Care for Disabled People," *Journal of Sociology* 40, no. 2 (2004): 137–55.

29. Brandon J. Griffin et al., "How positive processes function in negative relationships: Dispositional gratitude moderates the association between affective need and frequency of dating violence victimization," *The Journal of Positive Psychology* 11, no. 4 (2015): 388–398.

30. L. B. Aknin, E. W. Dunn, and M. I. Norton, "Happiness Runs in a Circular Motion: Evidence for a Positive Feedback Loop between Prosocial Spending and Happiness," *Journal of Happiness Studies* 13, no. 2 (2012): 347–355.

31. Liz Jackson, "Why should I be grateful? The morality of gratitude in contexts marked by injustice," *Journal of Moral Education* 45, no. 3 (2016): 276–90.

32. "Forgiveness: Your Health Depends On It," Johns Hopkins Medicine, accessed August 13, 2025.

33. Kirsten Weir, "Forgiveness can improve mental and physical health," *Monitor on Psychology* 48, no. 1 (2017): 30.

34. Feng Gao, Yuanwei Li, and Xuejun Bai, "Forgiveness and subjective well-being: A meta-analysis review," *Personality and Individual Differences* 186, part B (2022): 111350; Maureen Salamon, "Not just good for the soul," *Harvard Health Publishing*, March 1, 2024.

35. Suman Grigary Thomas and Shanmukh V. Kamble, "Forgiveness and Its Relationship with Social Connectedness and Subjective Well-Being," *International Journal of Indian Psychology* 11, no. 4 (2023): 2491–97.

36. Melike M. Fourie, Ruud Hortensius, and Jean Decety, "Parsing the components of forgiveness: Psychological and neural mechanisms," *Neuroscience and Biobehavioral Reviews* 112 (2020): 437–51.

37. Ervin Staub, "The Challenging Road to Reconciliation in Rwanda: Societal Processes, Interventions and Their Evaluation," *Journal of Social and Political Psychology* 2, no. 1 (2014): 505–17.

38. Desmond Tutu and Mpho Tutu, *The Book of Forgiving: The Fourfold Path for Healing Ourselves and Our World* (New York: HarperOne, 2014).

39. Aaron Lazare, *On Apology* (Oxford: Oxford University Press, 2005).

40. Elie Wiesel, *Night*, trans. Marion Wiesel (New York: Hill and Wang, 2006).

41. Jack Kornfield, *A Lamp in the Darkness: Illuminating the Path Through Difficult Times* (Louisville, CO: Sounds True, 2012).

Acknowledgments

I am blessed to have such an amazing circle of friends, family, and well-wishers to support me in bringing this book to you, my dear reader. I'm grateful for: Pervin's daily dose of love, laughter, positivity and awesome insights. Nil's love, support, intuitive listening, gentle guidance, and abundant generosity that made this book possible. Haresh's spiritual reality checks reminding me of my own power and who I truly am. Jodi, my soul sister, your love, laughter, joy, and play are a blessing. Lori, for your unwavering love and friendship. My Choti Moti, my play buddy, my joyful heart, for your constant love and adoration. Jillian, my Saraswati vak shakti. Thanks to each one of you.

I am grateful to my friends and family for holding me in your loving heart: Omi, Prabha, Shashi, Lalitha Devi, Jhummi, Kutu, Dinesh, Nonika, Rekha, Sanjiv, Sulu, Nitin, Sally P., Gail, Bina, Nagesh, Sanjay, Prati, Maria, Saran, Akshika, Dhruvesh, Rashi, Aditya, Suha, Dragon, Heidi, Michael, Ama, Tiffany, Vince, Ela, Chloe, Simran, Ronak, Amanda, Roland, Haejung, Agnes, Arleen, Franklin, Kurt, Natalie, Lisa H., Dharma Dancer, and many others.

Gratitude to my teachers: Amma, Premvarni, Jack, Raja, Sally, Andrea, Lila, Gina, Larry, Randy, Kathy, Peter, Layna, Stephen, and many others. My Spirit Rock friends: Anne R, Heather, Deanna, Maria Christina, Carol, Noli, Alisa, Solwazi, Kate, Kaira J, Victoria, Tere, JD, and many others.

I am deeply grateful to the KNLA team for skillfully guiding me to self-publish this book and making it fun: Amy Hosford, Jillian Abbey, Roger Copenhaver, Sheryl Zajechowski, Audra Figgins, Nicole Pomeroy, Christina Theile, Karen Sommerfeld, Tanya Casselle, Elisabeth Rinaldi, and Becki Ruh. Thank you for your care and support in making my dream come true.

About the Author

Pawan Bareja is passionate about helping people work with their trauma to step into a more joy-filled, resilient life. She has been a lifelong practitioner of meditation and mindfulness, with a focus on Vipassana meditation since 2001. Pawan is a graduate of the Spirit Rock retreat teacher training, a Buddhist ritual minister officiating weddings and baby blessings, and a community Dharma leader. She has educated thousands of students on healing trauma using mindfulness through her courses with Spirit Rock, San Francisco Insight, East Bay Meditation Center, and Esalen. Her teaching is infused with compassion, shaped by her own healing journey. For nearly two decades, she has served as a senior assistant at Somatic Experiencing trauma healing trainings and has traveled to India, her home country, to teach emotional resilience to professional care providers. Pawan also has her own private practice as a trauma resolution practitioner and works with a diverse population of clients. Drawing on practices that helped her during her own health challenges, she combines mindfulness and science-backed trauma resolution practices to help her clients work through the layers of trauma and shift into more joy-filled lives.

Pawan lives in Sedona, Arizona, where she fills her days with art, singing, dancing, hiking, yoga, and connecting with her Jungian and spiritual community. She loves being in nature and has hiked to the bottom of the Grand Canyon four times! She believes that cultivating love for ourselves and everything around us is at the heart of all healing.

www.ingramcontent.com/pod-product-compliance
Lightning Source LLC
Chambersburg PA
CBHW021230130626
46554CB00004B/1426